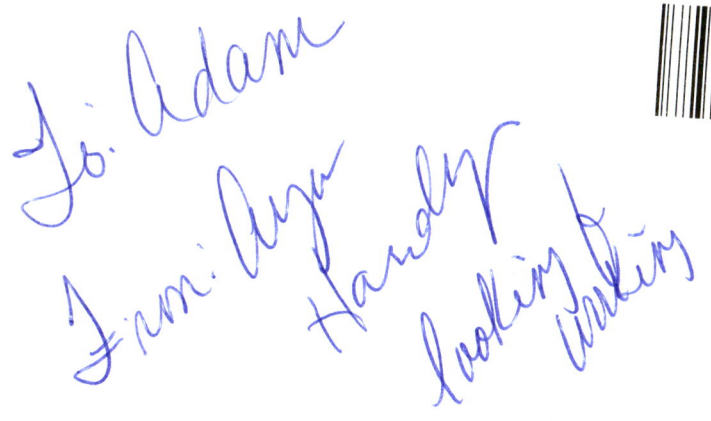

From Crack Mother to Wildflower

Writing To Transgress:
The Sankofa Writing Method

AYANA T. HARDAWAY, PH.D.

Copyright © 2024 by Ayana T. Hardaway, Ph.D.

Website: ayanathardaway.com

ISBN: (979-8-9901206-0-0)

All Rights Reserved. No part of this publication may be reproduced, distributed, or transmitted in any form or by any means, including photocopying, recording, or other electronic or mechanical methods, without the prior written permission of the publisher, except in the case of brief quotations embodied in critical reviews and certain other noncommercial uses permitted by copyright law. For more information on purchases in bulk or speaking events, please contact Ayana T. Hardaway at ayanathardaway.com.

Table of Contents

Introduction 1

Chapter 1 Theory as Healing Space 39

Chapter 2 Understanding The Sankofa Writing Method 83

Chapter 3 Remember to Talk Back 97

Chapter 4 Excavate Trauma 109

Chapter 5 Destroy the Myth 119

Chapter 6 Amplify the Margin 141

Chapter 7 Go Free, Wildflower 155

Closing Reflections 165

About the Author 175

Dedication

To my mother, *Tremayne*

My Grandmother, *Kathleen*

My Aunt, *Patricia*

My Aunt, *Marilyn*

To every 'Othermother' who saved me

To my girlchildren, *Jordan Nia* and *Ava Imani*

So you'll never have to wonder who your Grandmother *was*

Acknowledgments

This book is a product of my writing, deep reflection, and ideation over the last four years—but I would not have been able to do it without the support of many. I would like to thank my creator for the gift of having a long memory and a knack for writing while I reclaim my mother's story. To my husband, my best friend and partner in life, my protector, the yin to my yang—Nate Hardaway, for always encouraging me to speak my truth and chase my dreams. Thank you for always believing in me, even when I did not believe in myself. You have been speaking life into me for the last 14 years—and I am so incredibly grateful for your honesty, your compassion, and your support.

I would also like to thank my girlchildren, Jordan Nia and Ava Imani. Motherhood has changed me in so many beautiful ways. Everything I do, I do it for the two of you. My wish is that you will realize that your potential and dreams are limitless. No one can ever make you feel inferior without your own permission. What ceiling? The world is your playground to do and become whatever you aspire to be. Continue to walk boldly in your purpose, never compromise your integrity by shrinking for others, and always remember to honor your ancestors while doing so.

Gratitude to my brother, Ryan. My protector. My rock. My foundation. Our bond is indescribable. I would not be who I am today if it were not for you. Thank you for always taking care of me. I have and will always admire you, your charisma, your sense of humor, and your integrity. I am grateful for our companionship—and our shared life experiences as children being raised in our beautiful family. I am grateful for our inside jokes and shared interests. Through our pain, we snatched moments of joy with each other. I am grateful for the loyalty that we have toward one another—loyalty that flows through the bloodline. Brother—I am so grateful to be R.T.'s little sister. A badge of honor that has always yielded respect from others. Protection for a baby sister—as I navigated the streets as a girlchild. Life has not always been kind to us—for the things we have seen through our *child eyes*. For the things we experienced. But through it all, we have always had one another. Backs pressed against each other. Arms wrapped tight around one another. Hands clasped together—releasing our grips to wipe each other's tears—and laughing at one another's jokes. *Big Brother—Little Big Sister.* Unbreakable. Impenetrable. I see you. Beautiful Black man. Strength of a King. In this work—I honor you and our mother—insistently, unapologetically—to paint a more accurate picture of *our story*. I honor you through the recollection of memories from our youth. I have and will always honor you as I take on the privilege and honor of being an *Othermother* to your beautiful children. Unwavering loyalty flowing through the bloodline. Teaching them and modeling the rich cultural tradition of Black family values and pride.

I would like to thank my late *Aunt Patricia* and my dearest *Aunt T—* our family matriarch and *Othermother* to many. You are pure GOLD. Your grace, your poise, your eloquence, and your unequivocal loyalty to your family are admirable and otherworldly. Ever since I was a girlchild, I have watched you both—I have studied you, and through your lessons, I have learned to cherish and value family over everything. You two have taught me to love hard, and you have always encouraged me to keep growing. You have taught me what true Sisterhood looks like. Thank you for raising me as your own when your sister—my mother—was unable to.

As Tremayne's daughter, I wish to create space for you here to say the words that my mother may not have ever had the chance to express. Thank you. Thank you. Thank you. Thank you for loving Ryan and me—unequivocally. Thank you for loving our mother hard, no matter what. Thank you for taking care of her and showing her grace through it all. Thank you for your unwavering and unbounded support as you managed her medical and clinical care and never turned your back on her. Thank you for demonstrating to our entire family what loyalty as a sister looks like—salt of the earth. You are our teacher. Gathering us together and making corrections. Thank you for showing me how to see my mother's humanity and for creating space for me to express myself even when I simply could not see beyond my lived experience of being what sometimes felt like a motherless child. I honor you for your fervent and unbounded love. I love you beyond measure and words. I love you beyond the midnight sky. Thank you for loving me. Your *Yannie-pooh*. Thank you for keeping me.

I am grateful to the *Otherfathers* in my life. I was never a *daddy's girl*. I was always an *uncle's girl*. To my uncles: Bernard, Tyrone, Cassie, Terry, and Bikim. You each hold a special place in my heart—for showing up for your mother, father, and sister in such a painful and unexpected way. I thank you, and I honor you for raising the children when your sister was unable to—when she was not herself. And on behalf of my mother, I wish to say the words that she may have been unable to say. Thank you. Thank you. Thank you. Thank you for continuing the rich cultural tradition of raising the children—and extending grace to allow us to grow. Thank you for your lessons and for continually showing up and supporting my brother and I—no matter what. In this work, I rely heavily on my experiences with Black women centered networks—but I would be remiss if I did not acknowledge the role of Black men in cultivating a homeplace, expressing love toward the children, and protecting us in ways that we so desperately needed. I see you, and I honor your sacrifices as you raised your own families and considered us your *otherchildren*.

Gratitude to the entire Tyler family. Our family and our rich ancestry reflects a dynamic and unbreakable foundation. Willie 'Hank' and Kathleen Tyler did not come to play when they birthed an entire village. A village of strength. I love you all.

To my village, my sisters, my girlfriends, my Sorors, my line sisters, and my friends—I would go to war for all of you, and I am so grateful to have such a supportive network. I thank you for the space you created for me in your lives. I thank you for sharing in the experience of genuine friendships and love for one another.

Ubuntu.

As a scholar, I have many to thank for their continued support and encouragement concerning my research interests, theoretical ponderings, and professional development. I would like to thank my mentors and academic faculty who served on my dissertation committee at Temple University, **Dr. James Earl Davis, Dr. Novella Keith, Dr. Will Jordan, Dr. Jennifer M. Johnson,** and **Dr. Tiffenia D. Archie**. I honor you beyond your credentials, I honor you beyond your roles, I honor you beyond your titles, and I honor you beyond your positions within academia. I honor you as elders. Thank you for always seeing me, and for your continued support.

I would like to give a special acknowledgement to my book coaches, **Dr. Jaz (Jasmine) Zapata** and **Coach Julia Saffold** of *Motivational M.D. Publishing*. As a Black mother and daughter duo, I must say that it has been such a reward and honor getting to work with the two of you. I truly believe that for *this* story, it is no coincidence that I ended up in your writing retreat before knowing that you two were even related. To do the necessary work of centering Black women and writing extensively about mother and daughter dynamics in this book, working with you two was incredible; a necessary part of my healing journey. Thank you for your guidance, your patience, and your support as I engaged in this work. You made what felt like an impossible goal, manageable. For that, I am forever grateful. Thank you for encouraging me to go deeper in order to do the necessary work of empowering others while creating a legacy for my family.

My perspectives are heavily shaped by my lived experiences and by other audacious Black women scholars and intellectuals, truth-tellers, and disruptors. Some, whom I know personally, and others whom I do not know personally—but respect deeply and whose scholarship has had a considerable influence on me.

Black women intellectuals who I must name:

Dr. Lori Patton Davis: A Canon. My mentor. A beautiful mind. Your leadership and your scholarship moved mountains for Black women scholars like me. Your unapologetic approach to center Black women and girls in educational research was my north star throughout graduate school. Your work inspired me to tell the truth and to position Black women fearlessly in their rightful place—at the center. Thank you for paving the way and for encouraging me to *just write*.

Dr. Venus Evans-Winters: A prolific and audacious Black feminist scholar, Soror Dr. V, your *Write Like A Scholar Bootcamp* was my antidote as I pondered how to tell my mother's story over the last few years. I give gratitude for your scholarship and for writing *Black Feminism in Qualitative Inquiry: A Mosaic for Writing Our Daughter's Body*. Your approach to writing (and not writing) your daughter's body was a roadmap—and a blueprint for me in thinking about how to write about my mother's body in a way that would honor her as an ancestor. For that, I am forever grateful.

Dr. Cynthia B. Dilliard: Distinguished scholar. Master teacher. Another beautiful mind. *Endarked Feminism* helped me to breathe as a young scholar. In *Learning to (Re)member the Things We've Learned to Forget: Endarkened Feminisms, Spirituality, and the Sacred Nature of Research and Teaching*, I marveled at the way you captured the ethos of how we show up in our scholarship and praxis with a consideration for our *full selves* and our sacred knowledge—spiritually and culturally. Your scholarship enabled me to remember, recover, and move forward as I pondered how to reclaim my mother's narrative.

Dr. Saidiya Hartman: An icon. Scholar of African American Literature and Cultural History whose work in historical fiction is indescribable. Your examination of how historical trauma is remembered and transmitted across generations is insightful. I discovered your work through *Lose Your Mother: A Journey Along* *the Atlantic Slave Route*, and your writings on critical fabulation within *Venus in Two Acts*. It was your critical interrogation of the reproduction of violence through historical archival methodologies and your combination of historical research with fictional narrative and critical theory that gave me permission to continue to question and wonder how I could write up against the limits of my mother's truth and cross boundaries to rewrite her narrative.

Dr. DuEwa Frazier: An audacious author, educator, and poet—I thank you for granting me the grace and the space as an editor to write through my speculative ponderings about an *Endarkened Afrofuturist Feminist* epistemology and *Shapeshifting* as a methodology. Thank you for your encouragement and guidance as I navigated this publication journey.

Dr. Dorothy Roberts: A distinguished legal scholar and author of *Killing the Black Body: Race Reproduction, and The Meaning of Liberty*. Your scholarship centering Black women on racial justice, reproductive rights, child welfare, and social inequality tirelessly exposes systemic injustices and advocates for social change and equity and fuels me to dig deeper. Your scholarship gives me energy. Your scholarship answers my *what* and my *why*, when I think about the type of educational scholar I want to be, who and what I advocate for, and the reason why I write. I have always written to tell the truth, and your scholarship makes me evaluate my own research interests and the types of research questions I aim to ask. Your scholarship ignites me to act. Gratitude to you for this work.

Dr. Tanya Telfair Sharpe: A Black woman, truth-telling, public health powerhouse, research behavioral scientist and epidemiologist with the Centers for Disease Control and Prevention, and author of *Sex for Crack Cocaine Exchange and Poor Black Women*—while many scholars were doing research *on* Black women addicted to crack cocaine, you sought out to give our mothers a voice and engaged *with* them in the sharing of their narratives. You critically center Black women in their proper location, and you meticulously examine their behaviors and decisions through a cultural lens. You explicitly named the oppression while also writing their truths with the utmost respect and reverence. As a daughter-scholar of a mother who fell victim, your scholarship was healing for me—an incredibly important piece of our *(her)story* that details and names the violence experienced by Black women in the U.S. during the crack cocaine epidemic and genocide. As you state in your book: *"It became immediately apparent the poor black female crack users experienced the worst forms of social degradation and received the fewest opportunities for help."* Thank you for giving these Black women their voice to truth-tell from the margins.

To the dopest, flyest Black women—the Founders of the *Crunk Feminist Collective*, **Dr. Susana M. Morris**, **Dr. Robin M. Boylorn**, and **Dr. Brittney C. Cooper** —thank you for your brilliance in creating a space for Black girls like me to not only explore race, and gender critically through hip hop, popular culture, media, music, and literature—but for carving out spaces for us to show up as our full selves within the academy.

Dr. Susana M. Morris: It was your seamless blending of theorizing about Black feminism and Afrofuturism through speculative fiction that inspired me to consider how we might speculate and recover tools as freedom devices to protect ourselves right now.

Dr. Robin M. Boylorn: *Sweetwater* is exceptional—and your eloquent articulation of critical auto-ethnography as a method and mode of doing research on the self as a Black woman is insane!

Dr. Brittney C. Cooper: You snapped in *Eloquent Rage: A Black Feminist Discovers Her Superpower*! I am grateful for your lessons on how to articulate and use our rage as a transformative tool for asserting our agency while doing the necessary work of challenging injustices.

Dr. Stephanie Toliver: Your work centering on the Black imagination and the freedom dreams of Black youth in *Recovering Black Storytelling in Qualitative Research: Endarkened Storywork* was so beautiful and inspiring to me. As an educational scholar, your methodological contributions shaped my thinking about ways that we can perceive Black futurity to heal ourselves through storytelling.

Last but certainly not least—special gratitude to Black women *SisterScholars,* **Dr. Janelle M. West, Dr. Patrice S. Renee, Dr. Jennifer M. Johnson, Dr. LaWanda W.M. Ward, Dr. Nadrea Njoku, Dr. Musu Davis, Dr. Jamila Lee-Johnson, Dr. Sharron 'Shay' Scott** and all of the amazing Black women on the ***Mary Jane Legacy Project*** research team. You all are *fierce—truth-telling, pub writing, side-eye giving,* and some of the most brilliant scholar-practitioners that I have ever known. I am so grateful to be in a community with some of the realist Black women intellectuals on the planet. Thank you for your unwavering support as thought partners, listeners, confidants, collaborators, and *sisters.* Over the years, your integrity, scholarship, and leadership have been constant sources of inspiration to me. Black women are truth-tellers, and I carry you all with me as I envision new worlds under a new sun for Black women and girls in educational research.

Ase'

Wildflowers

Some of us lost our mothers twice.
We heal through Nommo.
We heal by rewriting our mother's stories.
We liberate our mothers by rewriting their stories.
We create space for them. Untold stories, in worlds (re)imagined.
We reclaim the narratives of our families. We reclaim
the narratives of our communities.
With lives lived fully. Untampered. Unabashedly free.
Rooted to the earth.

Wildflowers.

We take back the years. Stolen. We heal.
In the spirit of Sankofa, we remember remnants of their souls
and we (re)alive them.
Their voices. Their desires. Their pleasures. Their humanness.
Their ambitions before they were tampered with.
Their joy before they were violated. Their innocence before
they were robbed.
Before they were taken from us.

Wildflowers.

*We hear them as vibrations from their wombs where we lay nuzzled.
Heartbeat to heartbeat. The blood of our blood. We create new imagery.
Untainted. (Un)-Oppressed.
The act of replacing images of our mothers as 'crack mothers'
is a liberatory act.
We write to heal. We write to see them as the multidimensional
beings they are.
Seeing them and their possible futures.*

Wildflowers.

*We write for our Grandmothers to reverse and disrupt the pain they felt when they lost their daughters. We write for our Othermothers on bent knees, pressed towards the earth, while praying for their sisters.
We reclaim our power in creating space for our mothers.
Our sheroes. Our Ancestors. We create worlds where our mothers can live freely.
Beautifully. Unharmed. Untamed.
Wild and free.
Under a new sun and a willow tree.*

Wildflowers.

Introduction

*How simple a thing it seems to me that to
know ourselves as we are,
we must know our mothers' names.*
~ Alice Walker

My family and I were standing in our living room one Saturday morning, making plans for the day. We had just finished eating breakfast, and my daughters were playing. Two toddlers. Jovial and clumsily making messes where I had just cleaned up. After wiping down the dining room table, I stood there disheveled. Looking crazy. The news was on in the background—reports about protests and updates on the latest Covid cases in San Diego County.

Protests. Covid. Isolation. Toddlers. Pandemic.

I stood there in a daze, and suddenly, I caught my daughter Jordan's gaze from across the room. She was four years old at the time. I smiled at her. Signaling that she had my attention. I could see the questions forming behind her bright brown eyes. She was so curious. She was watching me. Studying me. She walked toward me, and then she asked,

"Mommy, who is your mommy?"

Her question caught me off-guard. I stared back at my daughter. She stared back at me. I hesitated and continued to stare back at my daughter. The silence was loud as I searched for a word. A fond memory. Something. Anything to articulate exactly who her grandmother was. My heartbeat swiftened as I scanned my memories and searched for a word.

What was I suddenly feeling? Was that nausea? Discomfort arose, and more seconds passed until I finally looked at my daughter and said,

"My mommy's name was Tremayne babygirl, and she was your grandmother. But sweetheart, she passed away many years ago."

My daughter looked back at me and replied,

"Okay," before swiftly running off to continue playing with her little sister, Ava.

She left me standing there. Completely undone. I stood still and absorbed the truth about the simple question my daughter had asked me. I realized that it was not a simple question at all. In fact, it was one of the most complex questions that I have ever had to answer in my entire life.

"Who is your mommy?"

I chose a safe answer. One my girlchild would understand. The conversation left me feeling uneasy, off balance, a little shocked and disappointed that I was completely unprepared for that moment. Surely, I knew that my children would ask me about their maternal grandmother someday. My daughter's question sent me into a spiral. I looked around my home and I realized, there were no pictures of my mother. There were pictures of our family everywhere—a host of photos from grandparents, aunts, uncles, and cousins. But not one single photograph of my mother. I had plenty of photos of my mother, but I kept them stored away in physical and digital photo albums. I looked at my mother's pictures often, but these stolen glances were for me and for me alone. I was creating space between my mother and my children.

Why?

Was I keeping her a secret?

Am I protecting them from something?

What was I protecting them from?

I pretended to act like I didn't know the reason. I recalled a few distant memories of sharing pictures of my mother with my daughters, but up until this moment, I never felt a strong desire to make sure they even remembered her name. How could I expect them to know anything about her? Why didn't I share my mother with my children more often? I answered my own question in my mind with a half-truth.

They are still young. You'll tell them about her when they're older.

But that wasn't it. There was something more. Other reasons why I kept my mother hidden. At that moment, I realized that I was responsible for my own mother's erasure in their minds.

That was four years ago.

****

The truth is that I did not have many fond memories of my mother. I couldn't share what I didn't have. I had many memories, but not many that I would describe as fond. In retrospect, I spent most of my young adult life suppressing childhood trauma directly connected to my mother's battle with drug addiction stemming from the crack cocaine epidemic and genocide.

Throughout my life, I was called *smart, resilient, and tenacious.* Deflection has always been my trauma response. I have always known that my "success" was rooted in intergenerational trauma stemming from my mother's addiction. There was never anything magical about my survival and my resilience. At least, that was the way that I saw it. I created a boundary a long time ago when it came to discussing my mom with anyone. I simply did not discuss her.

Come to think of it, no one else did either. Of all the people I knew with a parent or relative who was "out there," we didn't discuss it. The silence was always loud. We know why we don't discuss it. We don't discuss it because *mind your business*. It's painful. The ramifications of the crack cocaine epidemic and genocide are still very real to some of us. Whether it's broken families, poverty, the loss of life on the streets, or dealing with the removal of Black men in our communities stemming from the war on drugs and mass incarceration. The epidemic is over, but the implications of the Black plague are still very real. We don't discuss it *because we not only survived the unimaginable,* but some of us are *still surviving* it! And we're not defined by it. At least, I didn't think I was. I thought about starting therapy after I graduated from undergrad back in 2006. Back then, my hesitation was rooted in distrust and speculation about sharing my business with a stranger. Going to therapy was *"for the white folks."* My girlfriends were my therapists. As a matter of fact—we had therapy sessions twice a week. Once during happy hour, and once during Sunday brunch. Period. We were vaults for one another, and I trusted their guidance if I ever needed to vent or process anything about my mom, which was rare. I didn't spend much time at all thinking about my childhood. I learned to cope with chaos by staying busy. I never had time, let alone to sit and talk to anyone about my past. Who had time for that?

I was always out, *rippin' and running*. Growing up, my grandmother would yell at us.

"Y'all betta stop rippin' and running 'all up and through' this house."

I was fascinated with her word choice—the imagery she'd created. She was usually just talking about us coming in and out of the front door to go play outside. But in her mind, we were *"All up and through"* her house whenever she heard the front screen door shut. I knew better than to question her—I just loved my grandmother's way with words.

So, I spent much of my adult life ripping and running. Too busy to slow down and really reflect. Making good choices was a trauma response that I learned in my girlhood. I could see the pain that my mother's addiction caused my family, so I gave myself little room for error so that I would not disappoint them. I was also terrified of being disposed of or sent away. I also secretly wanted my mother's validation. I wanted to make her proud. So, I dedicated my dissertation to her. My feelings about my mother covered a wide spectrum. But they were mine, and mine alone. While I never let my trauma define me by wearing it on my sleeve, it most certainly informed my choices to do and become everything my mother was not and could not become.

I was always aiming to be *more*, so that I could redeem her behavior. Somehow, I thought that if I could just be a "good daughter," it would make what was happening to my mother seem less painful for everyone. Imagine that. High achievement manifested as a goddam trauma response. I never saw myself as a "survivor of trauma." I compartmentalized my mother's battle with addiction as something that happened to her in isolation of myself, and through my girlhood, I blamed her. So, as an adult, I just coped with it. I kept myself busy. Always ripping and running. Too busy to slow down and really reflect. I have time now. So, here goes.

One day in 1988, my mother dropped my brother and me off at my grandmother's home "down" North Philly and never came back to get us. Motherless children. As a four-year-old, my grandmother would always tell me that my mother was sick. So, I grew up thinking she had the longest cold ever. Sickness, to me, only ever lasted for a short while. It was like my mother was stuck in a place. Frozen in time. I stood by, waiting for her to become unstuck. I didn't want her to be sick. I waited for her sickness to pass so that we could be a normal family. It never did.

I can remember seeing my mother as a silhouette of a caricature. I was ashamed and sad as a little girl. Overtime, that would change to feeling abandoned and resentful. Oftentimes, I would ask myself, "Why me?" I wished that I had been born to someone else, anyone else. I did not understand why this was happening to her.

I am fortunate. My brother and I were well protected by our family. We were protected by our village. As a girlchild, it was my grandmother and my aunts who kept a watchful eye. Southern women. Sisters of the yam in distress for what was happening to my mother and what could happen to us because of it. They covered us—stretched their arms around us, squeezed us tight, and never let us go.

A lot of kids in my neighborhood experienced what we did. According to the United States Bureau of the Census, 3.2 million children in 1990 lived with their grandparents or other relatives, capturing a 40% increase over a ten-year period. Among Black children, between 20%-70% were believed to be in the care of their grandparents or other relatives. During the 90s, a lot of us were *"Grandma's Kids,"* which denotes a particular politic and point of view for Black Americans born during the crack epidemic between 1980 and 1995. While the scourge of the crack-cocaine epidemic and genocide ravaged Black communities and families across the nation, thousands of children were removed from their families and communities and placed into foster care. Some children were taken in by family members to carry on the tradition of child-rearing responsibilities because our parents were 'out there' and suffering from their battle with addiction.

In my neighborhood, this was normal. And we all moved forward.

We grew up in *Strawberry Mansion*, a neighborhood located east of Fairmount Park in North Philadelphia.

In 1948, my grandparents, Willie (Hank) and Kathleen Tyler, got married. My grandfather, a World War II Army veteran, and my grandmother moved from Shelby, North Carolina, to Philadelphia, Pennsylvania in 1954 during the second great migration. They made this move with their three children to find work and provide a better life for their growing family. Over time, they expanded their family to seven children.

My grandparents laid down roots in what used to be one of Philadelphia's most affluent areas. They were the second Black family to move into a predominantly Jewish neighborhood and block, which rapidly transformed into a predominantly Black community due to discriminatory government policies and housing practices within a single generation.

During the 1950s and 1960s, wealthier Jewish residents moved to the suburbs as part of the white flight phenomenon, resulting in economic decline and urban decay. This exodus left behind rowhomes that were then purchased by working-class Black Americans, who had migrated in significant numbers from the rural South—My grandparents, along with their brothers and sisters, were among this demographic, as they sought refuge from racial violence and oppression, and sought job opportunities in the city's factories to provide a better life for their growing family. My grandfather worked as a forklift operator for twenty seven years at Sealtest Dairies in Northeast Philadelphia, where he retired. My grandmother was employed by the Wagman Hair Factory for many years but before that, she was the neighborhood hairdresser. On holidays, including Easter, she was known for doing hair for adults and children throughout the neighborhood. She would charge her clients $3 per head as she worked magic with her curling irons on the stove. After leaving Wagman's, my grandmother was employed by Mrs. Paul's Kitchen in Northeast Philadelphia before she retired 20 years later.

Between their seven children, and a host of grandchildren, my grandparents also had family *all up and through* North Carolina.

You see, my people come from Shelby, Charlotte, Kings Mountain and Gastonia. So, we visited frequently. We traveled down South every summer in my grandfather's navy blue Lincoln. We always stayed down south for a few days each summer. Those trips were otherworldly. Always filled with connectivity. Roots. My grandmother would fry us up some chicken, cornbread, macaroni and cheese, and potato salad for the drive down 95'. We ate really well. We would hang with our cousins and stand in a circle, clicking our tongues and studying our dialects. We'd go around the circle saying different words. Trying to find out why they call all shoes, *"Tennis shoes."* Why they call it *"Livermush"* when it's really called *"Scrapple."* And why they called it a *"Beach tail"* when it's a *"Beach towel."* We couldn't understand why they talked and moved so slow, and they couldn't understand why we talked and moved so fast. It didn't really matter because we loved our cousins hard and loved spending time with them each summer.

We traveled to family reunions at least twice a year. We spent weekends rotating houses, staying with aunts, uncles, and cousins. After school and over the weekend, we visited the garden. Our grandparents, great-aunts, and uncles shared a piece of land that was our family garden near the Fletcher Street Urban Riding Club and horse stables. Yes—the same stables from the movie Idris Alba starred in called *Concrete Cowboy*.

You see, my people were plant scientists. Botanists. Southern people; farmers. So, when they moved North, they continued the tradition. We planted our own produce for our entire family, friends, and neighbors. Farm-to-table food in the middle of North Philly was happening in my home—*eating organic food before it ever became a trend*. My grandparents were working young folks—raising seven children, working their jobs, and maintaining the family garden. My grandmother was an oracle. A baptist, a spiritual woman who could hold her corn liquor, play the blues on the piano, and have Sunday breakfast and dinner cooked before 10 a.m.

My grandmother was a scientist. She played the lottery based on her own scientific formula. She played her numbers based on the numbers that came to her mind through her dreams. She'd wake up in the morning and study the numbers that came to her. She had a dark green dream book. I knew it was a good book growing up because it was worn. It was aged. Stained. Beige pages. Corners ripped on the edges. She kept that book on her nightstand, right up under her Holy Bible (Old Testament). She studied the numbers, and she would write them down in her book. Then she'd bring me with her on an errand to *Murry's* and then to play the numbers. I never questioned her methods—but it made sense to me because it made sense to her.

My grandmother was clairvoyant; she knew when the family was growing through her dreams about fish. When folks told her they were pregnant, she'd say, "*I know.*" Gifts passed through the bloodline. My grandmother was a healer. A *Shapeshifter*. People came to my grandmother's house to heal. No matter how you arrived, you would always leave my grandmother's house lifted, happy, joyful, with stomach pain from laughing so hard.

My Grandmother valued family. She was known throughout the neighborhood for her charm, and southern hospitality and she was infamous for her Sunday dinners. She welcomed any and everyone who stepped foot in her home with a warm meal and great conversation. A tall, thin, fair complected woman who made the meanest peach-cobbler and the thickest, most moist banana pudding that you could ever imagine. Mmm. Can't you taste it? She prepared whole meals in the blink of an eye and fed an entire nation. Family, neighbors, and children. Always sending somebody a plate. More gifts passed through the bloodline (just ask my girlfriends). My home, our home, was always filled with people—great uncles from Delaware, great aunts from North and South Carolina, cousins from New Jersey, Maryland, Texas, and Connecticut. So many cousins. In the Tyler household, there was always laughter, good food, great music and of course, dancing.

As a girlchild, I was fascinated with being around so many people whom I could call my family. The concept of having cousins who lived in other states and were also around the same age as me, was crazy! I loved it. Always cracking jokes. You see, my people are LOUD—we call things as we see them, we work hard, and we play harder because we deserve it. We have a good time. We gather for no reason—never needing a reason to celebrate. Our small home never *ever* felt small. It was always filled with people. Music playing, card games going, and drinks flowing. Kids would run up the stairs to put their coats away, food was everywhere, people were dancing, somebody was fussing, and life was being lived.

There were no wait times for dinner at Grandma Kat's house. If she told you to be at our house by 5 p.m., dinner was done by 3 p.m. Everyone knew to show up early. Reverse CP. Grandma Kat kept the party going—meeting everyone's needs. She took you in and fed you real good. Once she fed you, you became part of the extended family. I watched the elders convene as I listened to their stories about work, their health, their family. I absorbed different viewpoints from the elders who gathered at my grandparent's tiny row home in North Philly for Sunday dinner.

We gathered in small spaces but there was always enough room.

Every single person who ever walked through that front door loved us hard. And every single person would have something incredibly special to say about Tremayne, my mother. Memories exchanged. Family ties. Rooted to the earth. Spanning highways and area codes. My family did the best they could to fill every imaginable void. Everyone loved my brother and me hard and embraced us as children of our family. I viewed our family as a diamond in the rough. Always present. Loyal. Prayerful. Wrapping arms around us as *Grandma's Kids.* This is who we are—the Tyler's. Veterans. Innovators. Entrepreneurs. Creatives. Travelers. Musicians. Botanists. Farmers. Scientists. Doctors. A prideful Black family.

I breezed through school fairly easily. Making good choices and being a high achiever were my trauma responses. I gave myself very little room for error. I needed to speak up and learn all that I could so that I could become the smartest in the room. This was what my elders told me. I believed them. So, I moved forward. Swerving blatant aggression and microaggressions in early education settings. Dodging stereotypes and stigmas about my mother, and the fact that I was being raised by an Othermother.

I was teased and picked on by other kids in the neighborhood about my mother, and I was aware of popular culture stigmas associated with what it meant to be a "crackhead" and a "crack baby." The stigmas were everywhere growing up, and our family did the best they could to protect us from them. So we moved forward.

I spoke up often. Never felt intimidated speaking around the elders (when they allowed me to). I learned that from my great aunt Julia, who's pet peeve was listening to children mumble.

"Speak up, open your mouth."

If we were to say anything, we needed to sit up, straighten our backs, and say it with our chest. She had a little stutter, so I just assumed this was why she was always fixated on our speech. She also despised when we would chew our food with our mouths open.

"Chew with your mouth closed!"

I swear, each time I pop my gum, I can hear her cussing me out.

In school, I asked lots of questions of my teachers. I marveled at the knowledge their minds contained. My friends started to notice, and I would get asked to speak up for the class. So, I did. If we needed something collectively, I asked for it. I was good at organizing information. It never overwhelmed me. I was used to speaking with the elders growing up at Grandma's house. I was told that closed mouths don't get fed. The elders empowered me, never allowing me to shrink. Asking me questions. Asking me how I came up with my answers. Asking me about what I learned in school. So, I spoke up. I was also the little sister. My brother is three years older than me, but he always called me his "Big-little-sister" because I didn't care that I was little. I would speak my mind at every turn to stand my ground.

When I was in the sixth grade, my teacher persistently called me 'squeaky' in front of the entire class and told me that I talked too much because I was always asking her questions. I felt sad that she was punishing me for wanting to learn. Then, I felt bad for her because I knew my family. They would never tolerate a teacher teasing their *girlchild*. Eventually, I went home and told my grandmother, and she effectively confronted and cursed out my teacher, telling her never to call me out of my name again. My teacher apologized, and I continued asking her *all* the questions for the remainder of that school year.

I got called a 'leader' a lot but this was *never* a descriptor that I use(d) to describe myself. The way that I saw it, I was simply good at collecting and organizing information, and I wasn't scared to engage with the grownups. I recognized early that people in leadership positions had the information I was seeking. So, leadership is where I always ended up.

Leadership is knowing who and where the change agents are. I searched for the person who had the answers—I was always searching for the elders. I ended up "leading" because I could synthesize information. I was organizing data. I didn't become the President of Student Government (light flex) because I thought it was cool and would look good on a resume. I could have been doing other things after school, like going to South Street or the Gallery. I was there because I was nominated by my peers who trusted me. They knew that I knew who the change agents were in our school who could advocate for us.

I enjoyed finding solutions. I knew that my homies wanted a new Fruitopia machine in the cafeteria. Okay, cool. I overheard the underclassman saying that the DJ at the last party was trash. Okay, cool. We wanted more field trips, better lunch offerings, and programs that matched our fly. Okay, cool. Whatever it was, I was organizing data *with* and on behalf of my peers. Nothing changed in college. I ran with people who took over Executive Boards for fun. We *were* the change agents. We weren't sitting back and waiting for people to give us anything. We took it. We weren't doing it to get a shiny gold star. We were doing it because we were good at synthesizing information and organizing data. Our business was our needs, and I was just good at facilitating solutions. My elders told me to speak up. I believed them, so that's what I did.

During the 1990s, the Strawberry Mansion neighborhood was impacted by an economic decline, neglected by police, infested with urban decay, abandoned homes, lots, and businesses spread throughout the neighborhood. It was in these abandoned lots where I played with my brother and my friends. During the 1990s, our neighborhood had the lowest average home price in the city, coupled with the second highest number of violent crimes in Philadelphia. Schools suffered. The neighborhood was decrepit. Consequently, over the next decade, starting in 2000, our neighborhood witnessed a 20% decline in its population.

Nevertheless, our hood and our blocks were our homeplace, and I never felt or saw my neighborhood as unsafe at all. Through the lens of my girlhood growing up, those like my mom were peripheral players to a whole different world of Black culture and community. We were latchkey kids, and we were guardians of our homes and protectors of our family business. We knew to take the meat outside of the freezer when our grandparents weren't home. We knew not to tie up the phone line by calling our friends on three-way. As kids, we played all day. We were explorers of our neighborhoods, playing at Fairmount park, climbing the gates at The Dell Music Center, and we knew to be back on the block before the streetlights came on. We came up on block parties, fish fries, dollar hoagies from the pappi store, chopsticks in our hair, curb ball, playing jax, black lip liner around clear lip gloss, and hopscotch. There was nothing but bliss in my childhood—as the boys were out playing with their spinning tops, and the girls were sitting out front *'doing gimp'* showing off our latest designs:

Cobra twist

Butterfly

Box

Zipper

Circle

Snake around the pole

Our pastime activities stretched our imaginations. We were inventors. The streets made us, and Double Dutch was life.

Challenge, Challenge, One
Big Mack
Filet-a-fish
Quarter Pounder, French Fries
Icey Cola, Milkshake
Foot
Double Dutch was life
And as Blackgirls
The game was our teacher
The game was a portal for us to be whatever Blackgirl we wanted to be
Shapeshifting in the streets
Blackgirls grew wiser and stronger after an afternoon game of playing Double Dutch

Class was in session and we learned respect, life skills, social skills, confidence, responsibility, public speaking, time management, and negotiation
Deference was always given to the eldest Blackgirl
She was always the fly big sister on the block
If you were the youngest, you were stuck on the ends until you were told it was your turn
This was not to punish the young girls

*This was to teach the young girls to master the art of turning the rope
Because all the Blackgirls knew that to be a master jumper,
You needed to master the art of controlling and turning the rope first
Blackgirls teaching kinesthetic knowledge as prerequisites on the sidewalk
Using sensory feedback from bodily movements with our environment
to acquire knowledge, skills, and understanding
Double Dutch was our teacher*

*Girl Scout, Girl Scout
Do ya' duty, Cuz these are the rules you must obey
Salute to the captain
Bow to the King
Turn all around like a submarine
Double Dutch was life
And as Blackgirls
The game was our teacher
Faces covered when another Blackgirl said that she was 'paying'
Blackgirls teaching lessons about consequences under the streetlights
Teaching us accountability and how to take responsibility for our choices*

*We laced up our high top Reeboks, Nikes, Chucks and our KEDS
R-E-E-B-O-K
Do ya footsies the Reebok way
Street cred was given if you could jump real good
It was a light flex when the boys were watching
Nike Nike who can do the Nike
Foot to the N-I-K-E
We took breaks when the ice-cream truck came down the block
We made sure to remember each other's place in the game
Blackgirls teaching Blackgirls how to exercise long memories
We made sure to always ask our Bloodmothers and Othermothers
If we could 'please buy a new rope from the 5 and dime store'
We made sure to keep up our supply
My Grandma called them clotheslines
But us Blackgirls called them ropes
I knew better than to correct an elder,
So, I called them clotheslines too when I was speaking with her*

We were flip at the lip, quick-witted, and we grew hard exteriors
We popped our gum like the grownups
We cussed when the elders weren't watching
Shapeshifting
Becoming
Experimenting
Learning
Growing
Becoming masters of the artform
Double Dutch was life, and as Blackgirls
The game was our teacher

As a girlchild, I spent my days playing Double Dutch, and hand games like *Numbers, Miss Marry Mack,* and *Down, Down Baby, Down by the roller coaster*. Blackgirls playing hand games was a rite of passage. Coded messages teaching about culture, syncopation, rhythm, and how to exercise long memories. I was a talkative child. Always talking. In school. At home. Everywhere. Always walking around with a clipboard, taking imaginary notes, walking around in my grandma's high heels, her lipstick, and pearls—mimicking her and my aunties; *Aunt T* and *Aunt Pat*. My aunts did not play. They were always dressed to the tee. Always in business attire. Always reading books. They carried all types of books in their pocketbooks and read them on the Subway from City Hall to Fern Rock station. Fiction. Mystery. Science Fiction. Romance. Drama. They wore Avon and carried their magazines—*Essence. Vogue. JET. Ebony*. They ordered their jewelry and household appliances from *Popular Club*.

Black women reading books and seeking knowledge was familiar, and I aspired to be like them. They took those books from work to home and back again. They worked downtown, both in Criminal Justice. One was an administrator to a judge and worked in City Hall. The other one worked over on Arch street and was an assistant to the Chief Probation Officer. My aunts went to business school and modeling school. They were fierce—and they got the same lessons from the same elders who were helping to raise me.

Ignorance and stupidity were not options under the eyes of my aunts. They were sisters, and they were the oldest of the siblings—born only 19 months apart. My aunts were always taught to speak up, to go out and learn all that they could so they could become the smartest in the room. So, that's what they did. And they would tell me to do the same.

Lessons passed down through the bloodline. They worked for and alongside the smartest in the room. I loved going downtown and visiting the fancy tall buildings. My aunts taught us how to catch the train. Making sure we knew the difference between the *orange line* and the *blue line*. My aunts were beautiful and I admired them. My *Aunt T* called me precious and told me to always continue to learn. She was a human encyclopedia with a photographic memory. She remembered everything. An oracle. Always ten steps ahead. She wore her hair in a short stylish pixie cut, made the best home cooked meals, and gave me hot oil treatments during *wash day* when I was a girlchild. She never raised her voice, and she was (and still is) the most compassionate and caring person I have ever known. My *Aunt Pat* was also beautiful, and she was *always* raising her voice. She smoked newports, made the meanest potato salad, and taught me how to be brave. She taught me that it's a cold world, and to suck it up. She taught me not to be a 'stupid girl' and to use my brain to avoid making errors. She had a lethal tongue and could cut you down with her words. On sight. More gifts passed down through the bloodline. My Aunt Pat would go on about always reading the fine print and never trusting a soul. She'd tell me to outsmart everyone and to always protect myself and my family. Black women teaching the girlchild to take care of herself, seek knowledge and survive.

As kids, we were always learning. Lessons learned from our family, and lessons learned from the streets of North Philly.

My neighbor had the key to the water plug up the block. In the summer, we begged him to turn it on for us. He called it a fire hydrant. We knew better than to correct the elders. So, we called it a fire hydrant too when we were speaking with him. Running through that water plug were some of my best childhood memories. We had a neighborhood pool, but we preferred ripping and running through the water plug. As kids, we knew to mind our business.

You see, I didn't always feel like a motherless child because my mother was always there. I would run into my mother often when playing around the neighborhood. I learned to avoid her and any other person or distant neighbor who was 'out there.' Sometimes, I would see her engaging in *nefarious activities* with strange men in the park across the street from the playground on 34th street, where I would play with my friends. Stolen glances from behind the jungle gym. This was a normal day for kids like me. We observed, and we did not repeat what we saw. We minded our business. In those moments, I was terrified. Then I'd get distracted and continue playing, thinking only about what flavor of "Wooder-ice" I was going to get with my hot pretzel once we got back on the block.

We moved forward.

Sometimes, I would run into my mother on my way to school with friends, and these moments were always embarrassing because she always wanted money from us. Grandma Kat only gave me $2.50 for lunch money, so I never had enough to give her. Sometimes I gave her a dollar because, as my mother, I knew that I should help her. But overtime, I learned to avoid her by taking shortcuts. My friends and I would cut through the graveyard to avoid walking through the neighborhood. *A girlchild on the run from her mother.* I'd say a silent prayer for her in my mind, and I'd go along with my day. Moving forward. In my neighborhood, we made quick, snap decisions and always scanned our perimeter. We learned to move that way through the neighborhood, always watching our backs. We knew the corner boys. They were our brothers and *otherbrothers*. Protectors.

When I was in middle school, my grandmother would take me to Temple University on weekends for private flute lessons. Musical gifts passed through the bloodline. On the way, sometimes we would see my mother when we stopped by one of the rehabs she was occupying over on Broad and Dauphin street. She'd always hug me and smile—and then she would cry. Tears flowed where words could never form. Grandma Kat would provide my mother with bags of clean clothes, toiletries, and a plate filled with home-cooked food. A *Bloodmother* taking care of her girlchild.

We moved forward.

I did not wear shame on my face as a child, although I felt it. I tried really hard to mask it because the elders told me to speak up, to go out and learn all that I could. There was nothing that I could do. My mother was sick with what seemed to be an incurable disease—and it was in God's hands. My grandmother prayed for my mother every Sunday at Oak Grove Baptist Church over on 21st street. Sometimes, I could hear her crying and praying in her bedroom at night before bed. Tears dripping through the floorboard.

We moved forward.

My elders would say, "Chin up, baby girl," and my Aunt Pat told me to never let anyone question me about my mother.

She'd say,

"You tell them to mind their fucking business. And if anyone at that school has a question, you tell them to call me!"

"Yes, mam"

These are my people. My elders told me to speak up. So, I did.

****

I usually say what I mean and mean what I say. However, on this particular Saturday morning in 2020, my four-year-old daughter's question left me speechless. That was a rare occurrence for me. I could hear my ancestors yelling at me.

"Girl, speak up!"

Unknowingly, my daughter forced me to see that I was holding onto something that I've always carried with me. With one question—she became my mirror. Her reflection forced me to see my truth. She showed me that it was time to confront my trauma, and this was urgent! Because now, my girlchildren were watching me. I knew that soon, the questions would continue to pour in, and I needed to be unequivocally clear and firm about the narrative I believed to be true about my mother. For me, I needed to boss up and make a real investment in my mental health. So that's what I did. The only way that I knew how. I sought out a Black woman therapist immediately. There was no confusion about this once I started my journey looking for a trusted professional. Black women had always been truth-tellers and operators of my homeplace. So, I already knew that to talk through this pain-centering cultural trauma, only another Black woman would understand. The process was surprisingly really easy. I searched ThereapyforBlackgirls.com for providers who accepted my insurance. voilà! Within seconds, I had a list of local Black women who could help me navigate my mess.

Damn, so now I really had no excuse.

I scanned the credentials of the practitioners, and I chose one. I reached out to her office for a consultation and was placed on the waitlist that same day. Then boom, 30 days later, I was "in therapy." I had taken the first step toward my healing journey. This was by far one of the best investments that I had ever made in myself. It took me years to realize that to move forward, I had to release this shame that I was carrying with me internally all these years. Some call this *Shadow Work*.

So, I have done the hard work. And now, I am left with this gift that I am simply compelled to share. My goal is to empower, uplift, and inspire other Black women and second-generation trauma survivors like me to tell their stories and join me in this transformational healing journey.

I've always known that I was a writer. I wrote books as a girlchild. Writing was familiar. Interestingly—others seemed to know it too, because they would say it to me. I have a cousin named Melanie, who has been telling me that I should write my story for years. She thought that my story would be good enough to become a New York Times bestseller one day. Maybe one day. In all honesty, I don't think of my story as unique at all. In fact, there are many of us, hundreds and thousands of us, with similar stories—stories that we've also held onto inside because we simply did not know where to even begin to start telling them.

What I do believe is that our story is an untold one, which needs to change. The time has come. It is time for us to evolve. It took a long time for me to figure out exactly how I should enter this story. As scholars, we call this "the point of departure." This pain. It took years of maturity, and some living to really understand. My journey was long. The road to get here was long. The truths that I now embrace, I hope they can liberate others who have suffered from decades of resentment, shame, and trauma. Also, we don't need anyone speaking for us. If the story is going to be told, we can tell it our damn selves.

About Me

Real talk, I always despised writing my biography in the third person. The task always felt strange and alien to me. Just backward and counter-intuitive. Whenever I attempted to write one, it always felt incomplete. I viewed the normalized habit and practice as a fallacy. Biographies are, by definition, accounts of someone's life written *by* someone else. So why the hell would I write it in third person? That was a rhetorical question. We write them this way because we're "supposed" to. I've written a few here and there as a formality. In fact, I wrote one for this book. I wrote them as a snapshot and profile to share with my students and colleagues in academic and professional settings.

My point is that this normalized habit has always been in conflict with what felt natural to me. I believe that sharing this tad bit of information about myself tells you more about me than any bio ever could. So, in this space, I will not be spewing any fancy professional titles here or touting institutional affiliations.

To tell you who I am, I must first tell you who my people are, which I have just done. For the purpose of this book, I'll start by sharing that I am the daughter of a mother who fell victim and suffered for decades with drug addiction stemming from the crack cocaine epidemic and genocide, which was chemical and biological warfare waged against Black communities during the 1980's and the 1990's in the United States. As a result of this immutable fact, I am also a second-generation trauma survivor. My position as a Black daughter of a Black mother who fell victim is more relevant to this work and more important to me than any professional title, conferred degree, or institutional affiliation that I possess.

I will spill all the tea in this book, so I will use this space to humanize who I am so that, as a reader, you can get to *know* me authentically. I love spending time with my husband, Nate, and my daughters, Jordan and Ava (I refer to them throughout this book as my *girlchildren*). They are my homeplace. I prefer flats over drumsticks. I'm silly—an extrovert. I love wearing big hoop earrings and ruby-woo lipstick because there's something about this combination that triggers my *Black girl super power* and makes me feel confident even when I don't feel confident and reminds me that I am and will always be an *around-the-way girl*.

I'm a lover of music—gifts from my mother. I started playing the flute when I was in the fourth grade. By the time I was in the eighth grade, I was sight reading classical music—Mozart. Tchaikovsky. Bach. I'm a #CAPAKID. Class of 2002! We were the largest graduating class at the Philadelphia High School for Creative & Performing Arts at the time, and we were the first class to spend all four years in the new building on South Broad Street. Big flex! These facts matter, and collectively, we won't let anyone ever forget it.

I was first chair by the time I was a junior in high school. So good that I once played with the Philadelphia Orchestra. Also, first chair (humble flex). Music became my love language at an early age. I am obsessed with musicals. As a matter of fact, I still watch *Hamilton* at least once a month on Disney plus *because why is this even a question?* You don't? My family is sick of me because they know to move out of the way when Angelica Schuyler sings *Satisfied*, because the living room miraculously turns into the stage—and I become her. While standing there—in my bonnet and my robe, sipping my coffee. I'm a Soprano and love having concerts in my car. If you see me performing in these streets, *mind your business,* and please avoid contact.

I love reading and collecting books. Octavia Butler and Toni Morrison are my favorite authors. I'm a well-read jawn. Jawn is a noun. It is a word that we Philadelphians use to describe a person, place, or thing. On my cheesesteaks, I like *saltpepperketchup* (one word), mayo, fried onions, and pickles. I love to travel. I prefer romcoms and comedies over horror. I've watched every season of *Insecure* at least four or five times. I'm a member of Delta Sigma Theta Sorority, Incorporated, and I don't need to explain why. Spring 2006, Rho Alpha made.

My favorite dish to prepare is collard greens because my grandmother taught me how to pick them from our family garden when I was a girlchild. So, I teach my girlchildren how to prepare them as well to continue the tradition. I'm a doer. If I can think it then it's doable. I'm an Aries. I've always been direct. I moved across the country from Philly to San Diego one month after I defended my dissertation with my husband and two babies, who were only one and two years old at the time because we felt like it.

I take calculated risks when I know the return on my investment will be worthwhile. I'm a geriatric millennial. We don't age. I prefer day parties and being home by nine so that I can be in bed by 10 p.m. I love neo-soul music, burning sage, and lighting candles. I carry *Amethyst* in my purse. Swerving low vibrational people and activities.

I still bump *Floetic* like it just dropped. My playlist also currently has the following artists in rotation: *Ari Lennox, Alex Isley, Summer Walker, Anderson .Paak, Usher, Giminelle Mantra Loops, Snoh Alegra, Jhene Aiko, Jazmine Sullivan, Jill Scott, Erykah Badu,* and *Beyonce*. I love Jaz because *why is this even a question?* Her range is out of control. She's also a fellow #CAPAKID, and we used to catch the 32 bus together on our way to school. I love Jilly from Philly because we also hail from the same neighborhood and share the same birthday—also *Not Like Crazy* was craaazy! I love Erykah Badu because her music is a portal for us. She is also the baby whisperer—a spiritual Doula. So, of course, I played *"Ye Yo"* in my birthing suite on repeat while my girlchildren entered this world. Contracting to melodic beats. Hell yeah, I'm a member of the *B-hive* because who's not? I'm clumsy, so please don't stand too close to me or I might accidentally spill your drink. Don't worry, I'll grab you a tissue and I'll buy you a new drink. I collect scarves. All I ever wanted to be in this world was a writer. This is me.

I am also a transgressive and speculative writer, a creative, a futurist, and a scholar. I am a side-eye connoisseur, and I am usually unapologetically subversive in my writing about the (mis)treatment and suppression of Black women and girls in educational research. As a scholar, my research is situated at the intersection of critical qualitative methodologies, Pan-African and Afrocentric paradigms, Black womanist/feminist theory, and Black speculative literature. I am interested in using critical theory and intersectional scholarship to examine inequities and interlocking systems of oppression across social structures and institutions. From this lens, I name and examine oppression through my writing, and I situate the experiences of Black people as subjects and agents within the center of our own cultural, historical, and sociological contexts. There is truth in our lived experiences, and there is power through the spoken and the written word.

I am not interested in being palatable or politically correct when our lives and well-being are at risk. This is also me. This, dear friends—is who I am.

What Is This Book About?

This book is nothing like anything I've ever written before. This book is nothing I ever expected to write. In fact, I could not have written this book one year ago. This book journey has been a transformative and reflexive process for me. The writing method birthed through my healing journey is really a freedom dream and a byproduct of my radical imagination. This book is a love letter to my mother and a social experiment and effort to reach an entire generation so that we can heal. This project is about historicizing a moment in time from the perspectives of the children who were the first ones to experience having a parent/parents who suffered from their addiction to crack cocaine.

This book is a decolonizing project with the aim of sharing how I was able to take steps in my healing journey from intergenerational and childhood trauma stemming from my mother's drug addiction by *writing and imagining her free!* This here is quilt-work. Through storytelling, this project aims to weave communities and generations back together one stitch at a time. Quilting our stories continues the tradition of collecting our histories and preserving our legacies. This book is about deep-healing and reclaiming the stories of our ancestors through the *Sankofa Writing Method*, a method that I created to stitch myself back together.

This book is about facing our deepest fears and pulling up the roots of our shame. In the spirit of Black women literary scholars such as Audre Lorde, bell hooks, Toni Morrison, and Alice Walker, this book seeks to illustrate how writing and storytelling can provide restoration to Black women with imaginative maps to healing by writing oneself free. Through storytelling, I illustrate how we might change the narrative and create alternative futures for our ancestors as a method of resistance. This book provides a blueprint for how we might conceptualize futurity by reconciling traumatic historical realities while reclaiming the voices of our mothers, daughters, and sisters.

In this book, I weave together memories from my childhood as a self-healing literary practice to (re)imagine possible futures for my mother, one Black woman who was systemically disposed of during the crack cocaine epidemic and genocide. My aim is to disrupt the notion of the crack era as a taboo topic—a topic that, culturally, we avoid discussing because we find it offensive, embarrassing, or outright painful. It's time to unbury the past, find our voice, and spark new conversations about our healing so that we can move forward. It's time for us to evolve.

Creating Space for Grace

Let me be clear. I am not interested in comparing trauma. I am underwhelmed at the thought of debating stories of surviving the unimaginable at the hands of sustaining a white supremacist structure that subjugates our families and communities. As Black people across the diaspora, our business has always been our survival. We come from a long lineage of ancestors who survived Black plagues since the Middle Passage. Attempts to engage in any dialogue that positions us in opposition to one another are a distraction and do not serve us. My truth is my truth, and your truth is your truth. Attempts to compare our own trauma are divisive tools that create illogical divides within our community, which moves us away from our healing. What bonds us is our collective oppression and subjugation. This is rootwork, and our collective survival, despite our individual experiences, education levels, and socioeconomic status, is rooted in the same systems and structural policies that seek to oppress us. Healing is the goal. Speaking our truth is the goal. Creating space for grace is the goal. We must hold space that allows us to be free from guilt and judgment.

This project is about connectivity. This project does not seek to glamorize our survival. There is nothing magical or glamorous about our survival. Rather, the intention of this project is to create a safe space for healing through writing as a tool of resistance. The intention is for us to enter a conversation that we've avoided out of fear and shame. The intention of this work is to write through our pain, recognizing the power of the written and spoken word. The intention is to critically examine our beliefs and our mothers' narratives so that we may rewrite them, reimagine them, and reclaim them as our own. This project is about being brave, amplifying our voices, and recognizing our writing and radical imaginations as a practice of freedom!

Facing the Challenge

Centering our ancestors as victims is not without its challenges because it can be extremely difficult to forgive others who may have hurt us. The truth is, this is by far the most difficult and the most necessary step in the process. It requires us to confront difficult truths and reconcile conflicting emotions. Despite the pain they may have caused us, acknowledging our ancestors as a victim is the prerequisite for exploring alternative futures and finding compassion within ourselves. This journey cannot begin unless you are ready to see their truth. As we embark on this journey, we must also continue to consider the structural factors that contributed to our ancestors' experiences. Understanding the multifaceted nature of addiction and trauma allows us to view the issue from diverse perspectives. In embracing this perspective, we are called to adopt multiple viewpoints and embrace a nuanced understanding of our ancestors' journeys.

Who This Book Is For

If the contents of this book resonate with you, it is for you. I authored this book with a deep conviction inspired by The Combahee River Collective's 1977 proclamation that "*If Black women were free, it would mean that everyone else would have to be free since our freedom would necessitate the destruction of all the systems of oppression."*

The Combahee River Collective was a Black feminist organization active in Boston from 1974 to 1980. The organization was named after the Combahee River Raid, a military operation led by Harriet Tubman during the American Civil War, symbolizing the group's commitment to liberation and resistance. Black women saved me, so I have dedicated this book to them. Broadly, this book and the Sankofa Writing Method is for any person who has experienced the loss of a loved one stemming from cultural trauma. I also believe that by healing Black women, we can heal generations, restoring our families and communities. As such, I hold dedicated space for Black women so that we can learn to remember, recover, and move forward.

This book is for the Grandmothers and "Othermothers" who have shouldered the responsibility of carrying on the rich tradition of Black women-centered networks by taking over child-care responsibilities to preserve bloodlines.

Othermothering, fictive kin, and Black women-centered institutions are rooted in West African cultural values and traditions. This book is for any Black woman who continued the tradition and held families and communities together with collard greens and smoked turkey necks, hot water cornbread, Banana Pudding, support from her sister-neighbors, and a clothesline.

This book is for any Black woman who has survived her struggle through her own addiction on the journey toward recovery. For a woman who experienced losing custody of her child(ren), or for a woman who may find solace and catharsis through the language used in this text, which recognizes her victimization and calls out our collective oppression for what it is. This book is for mothers like Ms. Suzanne Sellers, Executive Director of *Families Organizing for Child Welfare Justice*, a nonprofit organization that advocates for child welfare justice and systemic reform. Ms. Sellers publicly shares her battle with losing custody of her children due to her own experience with addiction. In her open letter to the New York Times entitled, *Demonizing 'Crack Mothers,' Victimizing Their Children*, Sellers highlights how flawed science and racist media hysteria created the mythical moral panic that shaped the punitive legislation and public policies that targeted Black mothers like her; legislation and policies *which have yet to be repealed*!

Many of our Black mothers, Black sisters, and Black daughters were able to survive the Black Plague and the chemical and biological warfare waged against Black communities. However, many of our mothers, sisters, and daughters did not. Some of us lost our mothers *twice*.

This book is for my Sisters and Black women like me who are second-generation trauma survivors. Women who were born in the fire. Conceived in the trenches. Victimized and stamped at birth into a world that labeled us before we took our first breaths— reported on by major presses, such as *The Washington Post* as "better off dead," "monstrous babies," "the newest horror," "a bio-underclass," "crack babies," —a destructive caricature that remains etched in the American psyche, perpetuating harmful associations used to justify the violence and control of Black motherhood and Black bodies through criminal and reproductive oppression.

This book is for the daughters who weren't impacted in their infancy but who experienced the unimaginable and witnessed the destruction of their mothers, families, and communities firsthand. This book is for the Black girls who were still girlchildren, and suddenly needed to raise the children. I am writing for my Sisters. So that we may learn to look back, redress and reclaim our stories and our mothers' stories. I believe that as daughters, it is our duty to heal from this trauma so that we may reclaim our stories. It is our duty to heal from this trauma so that we may restore severed ties with our blood-folk and kin. It is our duty to heal from this trauma so that we unequivocally understand that we are worthy. It is our duty to heal from this trauma so that we may speak the life of our mothers to our sons and daughters. It is our duty to heal from this trauma so that we may do the real work of preserving and restoring our bloodlines. It is our duty to examine and question societal perceptions of our mothers and how these distortions have impacted us. It is our duty to recover the souls of our mothers by exercising discernment about how we think, feel, and speak about them. It is our duty as daughters to pull up and become the griots of our mothers' sacrifice so that we may preserve our genealogies and continue the oral traditions that we define for ourselves. It is our duty to heal so that we may continue the tradition. Ignorance and excuses are tools of the incompetent, and Black women cannot afford to be fools. This is excavation work that we must do. This is quilt-work that aims to restore and recenter our mothers at the center of their experiences as victims.

Sometimes, I go off. But I always bring it back. Stay with me.

As a scholar and a creative, I recognize that this writing method and topic might attract those serving in legal, public health, and helping professions. For those serving vulnerable populations, namely Black women suffering from addiction, there is power in culturally relevant interventions. Black art forms have always been a fundamental channel for addressing intergenerational trauma and promoting healing, as our history is marked by systemic racism and oppression. From a sociological and African centered perspective, examining the experiences of Black people without placing them at the center of their own cultural and historical context is inchoate, irrational, and illogical in any context.

The Sankofa Writing Method is imperfect, but I believe there is healing power in the imagery we create in our minds and the counter-futures that we express through the written and the spoken word. For my fellow scholars and academics, the crack cocaine epidemic and genocide needs to be studied. For my fellow scholars and academics who are also second-generation survivors of trauma, you are not alone. Your perspectives are needed. The silence is too loud.

Navigating this Book

This project is about speaking our truth and developing the tools to rewrite our stories free from the white gaze. We are not here to talk around the issue or to treat the crack era or our cultural trauma as taboo. We're done with that. Our truth resides in our pain, and collectively, I believe that something beautiful can be created on the other side. This book is structured as a guide, filled with practical exercises and writing prompts so that you too may join me in the journey toward healing.

Each chapter outlines the steps you will take in your transformational healing journey. This book captures a combination of my memories, thoughts, musings, poems, journals, artifacts and photos of my mother, conversations with other Black women who knew my mother, and life notes (written and recorded) over a three-year period. Throughout the book, I thread together memories of my life to track how I came to this work and how to apply the Sankofa Writing Method. Sometimes, I felt compelled to write a journal entry. Sometimes, my writing started off as a free-write, and organically—the cadence shifted into poetry. This is truly a creative process.

I wrote this book with the intention of rewriting my mother's story; however, I realize that not everyone has lost a mother, and not everyone has had someone suffer from an addiction to crack cocaine. This writing method is simply a tool, a bridge, and a transformative device that takes us from a space of shame and fear stemming from traumatic experiences to a space of empowerment, where we can reimagine and reclaim our stories while healing. Throughout the book, I will switch between the terms 'mother' and 'ancestor' to describe any person or victim who is the subject being centered in this work. I developed this method specifically to help those impacted by some form of cultural trauma. However, I will reference information and education about the crack cocaine epidemic and genocide since I am using myself and my personal experiences as the subject.

Lastly, we Black scholars are bilingual—we have range. We speak our mother's tongue, we listen to trap music, we have advanced degrees, and we use both necessary and unnecessary academic jargon to demonstrate our scholarly dexterity. To my folks, my village, and my family who are reading this book—I will code-switch throughout the text. In Chapter one—I will use lots of academic phrases and words so that I may do the necessary work of theoretically naming my practice. This is necessary. This is not a traditional scholarly book—I prefer it this way. However, I am a scholar, who is seeking to speak with other scholars outside of a traditional academic space. Consider this space the group chat. This project is for my mother, my children, my nieces and nephews, my family, my community—for people who couldn't give a damn about reading a peer-reviewed journal or scholarly text.

Exhale

I meditate now. This is new for me. I'm a beginner, but I am so grateful for the calm that meditation has given me. I thought meditating was strange before. I thought it was weird. I didn't understand it. Now, I do. So, I pay attention to my breathing. I breathe through my stress. I breathe through my anxiety. I breathe through the moments when I have completely broken down in tears—which happened a lot while writing this book. So, there will be moments throughout this book where you'll see me write the word *"Exhale."* This process is raw, and I want you to see my vulnerability so that you can give yourself permission to be vulnerable too.

Whenever I "Exhale" throughout this text, I am capturing a non-verbal emotion during a moment where I needed to pause, stop writing, and breathe. These were the moments when I had to let out a scream or a cry. It was a moment where I had to concentrate on my breathing so that I could calm my nerves. It was a moment when I had to stop writing and take a walk. The process of writing and the actual writing are one and the same. Writing through my pain was transformative, and it is important for you to *see* my truth. Acknowledge these very real moments.

Consider writing out the words "Exhale," "Break," or "Pause" to capture this emotional response as *part* of your writing process. In qualitative research, we call this "thick data"—which is contextually rich and detailed information that provides deep insights into human experiences, behavior, and social phenomena. "Thick data" adds texture - *seasoning* - and these moments are just as important to capture. Later, it will be powerful to see (on a page) how your emotional responses were woven into your writing throughout your healing journey. Trust me.

Writing Preparation

In addition to writing in a journal, you might prefer typing out your entries digitally. I have also found using audio recording apps on my phone to be easy and highly effective. Whether you're juggling childcare, work, school, or household responsibilities, recording your thoughts in real time can be a practical alternative when you don't have time to sit and write, especially as new ideas come. Once recorded, you can either transcribe the audio into your journal or utilize transcription services. Embrace technology as a tool to help you articulate your thoughts and ideas. The essence of this practice is finding your voice, capturing it, and preserving it for your own benefit. Experiment with recording your thoughts during mundane activities like your commute home from work or your morning coffee run to Starbucks. These spontaneous moments of insight are valuable, and recording your reflections as they come will ensure they are not lost.

Creating a Sacred Space for Reflection and Creativity

You will spend lots of time reflecting on your healing journey. Set aside a designated area in your home dedicated to deep reflection, writing, prayer, and meditation. Consider incorporating elements such as an ancestor altar, plants, candles, incense, and music to cultivate an atmosphere conducive to introspection and creativity. This space should be free from clutter or distractions and evoke a sense of tranquility. Prioritize comfort by choosing a cozy spot where you can fully immerse yourself in your thoughts and creative pursuits. Consider writing near a window for moments of natural sunlight or fresh air. Wear comfortable clothing that allows you to relax and focus without any unnecessary discomfort. Do whatever suits your fancy. My space actually includes all of the above and a little extra because, like Tab said, "*That's my business.*" My ancestor altar holds pictures of the Black women who saved me. My mother Tremayne, my grandmother Kathleen, and my aunt Patricia. For me, writing requires their presence. I honor them, and in my darkest and deepest moments of reflection, they propel me forward. Reminding me who I am. Do what feels natural and organic for you. By intentionally preparing this space, you can enhance your writing practice, fostering a deeper connection with yourself and your ancestors.

Definitions

Throughout this book, I will use terms that highlight key concepts about the Sankofa Writing Method that will be helpful as you navigate through the chapters:

- *Afrocentricity*: A theory and methodology developed by scholar Molefi Kete Asante, which centers on the experiences of Black people across the African diaspora within their own cultural, historical, and sociological contexts.
- *Counter-Future*: The concept of "counter-future," through the Sankofa Writing Method, is a narrative that embodies a form of resistance, critique, and creativity to reshape societal trajectories toward more desirable outcomes. This concept refers to alternative visions or narratives of the future that diverge from mainstream expectations, encompassing ideas that challenge prevailing norms, ideologies, and structures.
- *Crack Cocaine Epidemic and Genocide*: The "crack cocaine epidemic and genocide" refers to a period of widespread addiction, social devastation, and violence during the 1980s and 1990s across the United States. The term "epidemic" is used to describe the widespread and rapid eruption of crack

cocaine, a potent and highly addictive form of cocaine, particularly in urban areas. The term "genocide" refers to the deliberate, structural, and systematic destruction of a group of people because of their ethnicity, nationality, religion, or race. In this context, "genocide" refers to the devastating impact that the crack epidemic had on Black communities, especially in inner-city neighborhoods, which disproportionately targeted and harmed Black individuals and communities, leading to significant loss of life, mass incarceration, and the destabilization of families and neighborhoods.

- *Critical Traumatic Incidents*: Memories and experiences that elicit a trauma response stemming from direct or indirect exposure to traumatic events.
- *Cultural Trauma*: Cultural trauma refers to the collective psychological distress experienced by members of a community or society because of a significant and distressing event or series of events that profoundly affects their identity, beliefs, and values. Examples of traumatic events include colonization, forced displacement, genocide, natural disasters, war, or other forms of systematic oppression and violence. Cultural trauma often leaves a lasting impact on the collective narratives and memory of a community, influencing social and cultural practices, behaviors, and beliefs for generations to come.
- *Endarkened Afrofuturist Feminism*: Adapted from Black Feminist Scholars, Cynthia B. Dilliard and Susana M. Morris, *Endarkened Afrofuturist Feminism* is rooted in Black feminist theory. Within the subgroups of Black speculative fiction and Afrofuturism, *Endarkened Afrofuturist Feminism* is introduced as a critical epistemology to explore theoretical implications for using speculative and literary text to recover decolonizing technologies that can be employed for the success and liberation of Black women and girls.
- *Freedom Technology*: Tools used to resist oppressive conditions that enable us to survive our present realities.
- *Girlchild/Girlchildren:* Through this text, I use the terms "girlchildren" and "girlchild" intentionally to refer to

young Black girls as children and to reject any premature imposition of adult characteristics or stereotypes onto them. These terms emphasize the importance of recognizing and honoring the innocence, vulnerability, and need for patience and non-violent responses in addressing the behavior of Black girls within societal and educational contexts. These terms also counter implicit biases and societal pressures that may lead to the adultification of Black girls, ensuring that they are not unfairly judged or misunderstood based solely on their intersectional identity.

- *Homeplace:* Throughout the text, I reference "homeplace," which is a concept explored by bell hooks in her essay titled *"Homeplace: A Site of Resistance."* She uses this reference to describe sites of resistance for marginalized people as a source of strength and power.
- *Intergenerational Trauma*: Occurs when the psychological and physiological effects of trauma are passed down between generations.
- *Quilt Work*: This reference captures a method of archiving the Black experience through writing and storytelling that honors the tradition of quilting in the Black community, which serves as a powerful symbol of survival and resistance. Quilting is more than a craft; it's a ritual of communal resilience, allowing Black women to overcome oppression and reclaim their stories, connecting with their heritage and conveying urgent messages of empowerment.
- *Shadow Work*: Refers to a process of introspection and reflection aimed at exploring and understanding one's past experiences, emotions, and suppressed traumas.
- *Sankofa*: A West African word with origins from the Akan tribe in Ghana, which translates to "To go back and fetch it" —symbolizing the importance of remembering and obtaining knowledge from your past to move forward.
- *Shapeshifting:* A form of *Freedom Technology* and decolonizing speculative method of resistance that defuses any real or perceived threat to one's psychological and physiological state within any context. *Shapeshifting* engages both

spiritual consciousness and Indigenous knowledge and is exercised through deliberate control of one's own body through imaginative and literal actions as a method of resistance, self-definition, and survival.

Lastly, you are not alone, and I am here to coach you and guide you each step of the way. My hope is that this healing journey will result in profound quilt work, allowing us to metaphorically patch ourselves back together and acknowledge our ancestors as the victims they truly were. We must excavate the roots of our shame and critically examine societal perceptions that have impacted us so that we can reclaim our narratives. The Sankofa Writing Method changed me. I know this to be true because I no longer carry shame. I no longer blame my mother for the things she's done, and for the first time in my life—I realize that my story no longer belongs to me. Now, I track my life's journey to serve as a testimony for others to heal. Will you join me?

Through the Sankofa Writing Method, let us begin the transformative process of healing, self-discovery, and empowerment while reclaiming the narratives of our ancestors and our mothers.

Affirmation Statement
I am no longer carrying shame.
Shame has no place here.
I release shame.

Chapter 1
Theory as Healing Space

It is not easy to name our pain, to theorize from that location. I am grateful to the many women and men who dare to create theory from the location of pain and struggle, who courageously expose wounds to give us their experience to teach and guide, as a means to chart new theoretical journeys. Their work is liberatory. It not only enables us to remember and recover ourselves, it charges and challenges us to renew our commitment to an active, inclusive feminist struggle... Our search leads us back to where it all began, to that moment when an individual woman or child, who may have thought she was all alone, began a feminist uprising, began to name her practice, indeed began to formulate theory from lived experience.
- bell hooks

As a girlchild, I relied heavily on my imagination to see myself existing in other worlds. I've always been someone who developed abstract ideas about a particular subject to explain it. I've always studied others and phenomena around me. Growing up, I would sit on the front steps of my grandmother's home, daydreaming and wondering. Imagining. What would my life be like if I had a mother who was present? What would our world be like if my mother wasn't sick and stuck in a place? I wondered if others like me also *thought* like me.

Years later, I found another Black woman who felt the same way that I felt when she was a little girl. I discovered a legend—a Black feminist scholar, author, activist, and poet by the name of bell hooks, who talked about theory as a healing space, describing it as a sanctuary for introspection and transformation. It was through her work that I realized that I also had been theorizing all along as a girlchild. I had no idea that this was what I was doing, but I found connectivity in her writing when she described it in *Teaching to Transgress: Education as the Practice of Freedom*:

> Living in childhood without a sense of home, I found a place of sanctuary in the "theorizing," in making sense out of what was happening. I found a place where I could imagine possible futures, a place where life could be lived differently. This "lived" experience of critical thinking, of reflection and analysis, [became] a place where I worked at explaining the hurt and making it go away. Fundamentally, I learned from this experience that theory could be a healing place. (p. 61)

I always found solace in imagining alternative realities. In retrospect, I think a lot about all that I've gained by being raised in a village. I was a sponge, and I absorbed different ways of knowing from the elders. It was my grandparents, aunts, uncles, great-aunts, and great-uncles who molded me. Telling me that I could do and be anything that I wanted. They told me to speak up, to go out and learn all that I could so that one day, I could become one of the smartest people in the room. I believed them. So, I used theory not only to escape in my mind but I dared myself to find the pathway and solution to create whatever I could conceive of.

I was journaling one day, and I remembered how I grew to love storytelling as a child. I was always listening to the elders telling their stories from the deep South: every person was a distinct character in my girlchild's eyes. The elders would sit at the dining room table playing Pokeno. Sipping brown liquor from their glasses. Oldies blasting from the speakers. Plenty of food on the stove. Talking about the "Good ole' days."

One of my favorite storytellers was my neighbor, Miss. Tonya. She would tell the most amazing stories, with imagery so vivid that you felt like you were walking right up alongside the characters in her story. When my mother was not around, I was in the company of so many who taught me different ways of knowing and understanding the world. Black women gave me what my mother could not. Miss Tonya was at the top of the list of people who taught me how to wonder. So, I wrote about her:

Big Dipper, Little Dipper

When I was a young Blackgirl playing on the block
At night, my next-door neighbor Miss Tonya would sit on the front steps
And tell stories to the children
She was like a big sister on the block
She had thick, long black hair that she kept braided up in two plats on each side
She walked with a little limp
Sometimes she sat in a wheelchair
She carried a fly swatter, and she was smart
She drank homemade iced tea with lemon, and gave us candy
All the little black girls would gather on our front steps to listen to her stories
It was a convening, and our front steps were *the meeting place*
A time to wish, wonder, and learn
Squeezed tight, real close so we could hear every word
Sometimes, she would tell us stories with books
My favorite were the ones she told with no books at all
The ones she read from her mind
She was Black and 'had Indian in her family'
Cherokee
She talked about the stars and the planets
Atoms, and dinosaurs
Herbivores, and ocean life
How to play Uno (our way)
She taught us etymology, and to choose our words wisely
Molecules, and gravity

Big Dipper, Little Dipper

She taught us about pride and courage
She taught us to ask questions
She taught us to study hard so that we could gain knowledge
She taught us to be the smartest in the room

Big Sister, Big Sister

She looked after the children on the block
She kept a sharp eye out for the girlchildren

Little sister, Little sister

She always kept eye
Sitting on that step
It didn't matter that she couldn't walk real good
She knew everything that happened on the block
She was an alchemist
At night, she became our master teacher
A keeper of stories
Stimulating our prefrontal cortex
Planting seeds of ideation
Inquiry rising
She was a healer
Taught us how to solve problems with our thoughts
Asked us to imagine what the sun looked like in the dark
Taught us about the elements and chemical reactions
Told us to never let the boys and grown men touch on us
She told us that she would carry our secrets, so they didn't weigh us down
So, we told her everything
So that we could walk easy

Little Sister, Little Sister

She qualified our secrets, organizing data

Making decisions about actions and inactions
Cuz her Mamma, Ms. May told her to keep a watchful eye over the girlchildren
Ms. May told her daughter that she would carry her secrets, so they didn't weigh her down
So, Miss Tonya told her Mamma all her secrets and ours, everything she observed from the day
Sittin' on that step
And Ms. May called my Grandma Kathleen next door
And Grandma Kathleen called Ms. Pauleen from across the street
And Ms. Pauleen called Ms. Jonnie Mae from up the way
And Ms. Jonnie Mae called Ms. Gladys across from us
And Ms. Gladys called Ms. Laws down the street
And Miss Laws called Ms. Dolores on the corner

Blood Mothers, Othermothers

The women gathered in their meeting place
At their kitchen tables on 3-way
Twirling phone cords in one hand
Smoking a cigarette in the other
Dinner on the stove, flame on low to keep it warm
Taking names and collecting glances from the curtain
Exchanging information, and strategizing corrections
While the girlchildren were out on the front step learning about

Big Dipper, Little Dipper

This network of Black women were operators of our homeplace
Miss Tonya kept a watchful eye
She helped us access our superpowers
Through storytelling, she taught us fables and folktales
Fairy tales and not quite fairy tales about seeing spirits in the stairwell of her house
Hovering over burgundy carpet
Smelling the sweet scent of cigars and whiskey suddenly
And the lights flickering

'These were the ancestors,' she'd say – *'just an uncle passing by - nothing to be afraid of'*
We believed her, so we were unafraid
She continued with her stories about the stars
A constellation connoisseur
An astrologist
One night, as the Black girls gathered at *the meeting place*
She told us that the Little Dipper is where we could find Polaris
A very *shiny*, special star
The girls grew giddy

'Oooo, who is Polaris? Who is Polaris?'

We squealed - anxious to learn more about this new character

'Polaris is the North Star, and she sits at the handle of the Little Dipper'

We gasp, our jaws hit the floor! Big wondrous eyes, wide-eyed with excitement

'Whaaaaat?!'

Every Black child growing up in the 90s knew of the North Star
We knew to search for the North Star to find our way home
Textbook math
The North Star was our Global Positioning Symbol
In the summertime, while driving back to Philly from 'Down South' on 95, I searched for the North Star often from my window in the back seat
Slipping and sliding on a stack of yellow pages
I always knew my way home
I couldn't believe it!
Polaris was thee North Star!
The same star that led Harriet Tubman to freedom
Every Black child knew that Harriet led our ancestors to freedom
So, Polaris is the star who shined a bright light for 13 trips and 70 lives?

I couldn't believe that thee North Star was also "My" North Star
Even better, now she had a name
Miss Tonya talked about stars
Like they were something that we could just reach up and pull right up out the sky
She told us that we could, and we believed her
So, we did
We cupped the stars in our palms
Feeling their warmth
Twirling them around
They never felt as heavy as I imagined
She taught us to see the stars the way we wanted to see them
I thought a lot about Polaris

Eyes closed; I imagined her as a Black woman

Because what other kind of star would shine a light so distinctly bright for 13 trips and 70 lives
What other kind of star could match her frequency
What other kind of star could command such reverence, ethereal and wise
What other kind of star could carry Little Dipper to guide Harriet to freedom
13 and 70 slaves
Connecting constellations to Black liberation

Little Dipper, Little Dipper

What other kind of star could have assumed a most righteous position
Channeling coded maps to the planet

North Star, Favorite Star

Keeper of secrets, watchers of the children
Black women were the operators of our homeplace
And Polaris was a Black woman who *Shapeshifted* into a star

Little Dipper, Little Dipper

She's so brave
And there I was, facing Polaris
I said *'So, you're the mighty North Star. How mighty you had to have been to carry that light for our ancestors all alone. How mighty you are, celestial and brave'*

Polaris looked at me, and smiled
Leaning slightly to the left, glancing over her right shoulder
So that I could see the truth
Big Dipper was right there behind her, a cluster of SisStars
Polaris said, *'I was never alone, because my Mamma is always here. You must find Big Dipper to find me'*

Big Dipper, Little Dipper

Big Dipper was a cluster of Black women
Polaris' Bloodmother and Othermothers
Keeping a watchful eye over their star-child
SisStars to other constellations exchanging information on 3-way
Creating coded maps in the sky using zodiacs
Telling Polaris that they'll carry all of her secrets, so they didn't weigh her down
So, Polaris told Big Dipper everything
So that she could shine her bright light without strain
For 13 trips and 70 lives

I opened my eyes,
Sitting next to Miss Tonya
Sharing my daydream about Polaris
Staring up at the Black night sky
Wishing
Hoping
Longing to one day have what Polaris had

Big Dipper, Little Dipper

My journey through theory has always been a way to escape—a way to understand what was going on around me. The way that I saw it, Black women *were* the operators of our homeplace. So, I imagined them that way. As a child, I created a framework for understanding Polaris. I told Miss Tonya that the stars were Black women, and she looked at me and smiled.

She said, *"That's highly possible."*

I replied with a smile, *"I know."*

Because I did know. This was my truth, and it was never up for debate. Because why wouldn't that be the case for Polaris, the North Star? Why wouldn't she be protected by Black women in the midnight sky? It was this speculation and mapping to understand our connections to the stars that I always did in my mind. To me, it made perfect sense. And this is precisely what theory was—it was sensemaking, and I marveled at the way scholars came to describe ways of knowing.

In undergrad, I always enjoyed sociology and learning about theory. What I perceived to be challenging for others came easy for me. I was fascinated with studying structures as constructs. I loved walking around campus saying Bourdieu's name and occasionally sprinkling the word *habitus* around like pixie dust during conversations with my friends on the quad. I absorbed theory, and critiqued it. Just like Miss Tonya taught me to do, I'd pull theoretical frameworks out of the text, and I'd hold them in my palm, studying them. I was searching for my story in their frames. I did not always find them. But it didn't matter because I was a *Black girl belonging*. I made myself know even when I didn't care. I *Shapeshifted* and I made myself belong. Because my elders told me to speak up, to go out and learn all that I could, so that one day I could become one of the smartest in the room. I believed them, so that's what I did.

In grad school, I majored in Urban Education and studied brilliant scholars of critical pedagogy, like Barbara Sizemore, Paulo Freire, bell hooks, Gloria Ladson-Billings, Pedro Noguera, and Peter McLare—each offering unique perspectives on the sociology of education, social justice, and transformative teaching practices. I moved forward. Training, seeking, and dissecting methodology. I was heavily influenced by critical theorists and The Frankfurt School in those early years. There was always something missing for me, as a Black woman, and my ability to connect to these white men and these other ways of knowing. But I learned it anyway because I had to.

Twirling circles around epistemology and contemporary trends in educational research. Holding hands with hermeneutics and the interpretation of language and the art of communication, because baby! This was fascinating! Swerving through intermediate statistics, higher educational economics, and finance. Basked in the connections made between urban schools and community partnerships. *Ubuntu.*

I absorbed all of what qualitative methodology could offer me because I found my soulmate. Line dancing with ethnography and taking strolls with critical phenomenology. Holding all of theory in the palm of my hand, examining, trying it on, stretching it out, critiquing, and then critiquing my own critiques of a thing. Mastering the etymology of words so that when I make my arguments, I leave no room for debate. Citational ninja. I marveled at how I knew what I knew. Critical theory was my sweet spot. I recognized this work—I was drawn. It was a French philosopher by the name of Michel Foucault whose work intrigued me the most. Foucault resonated with me because he occupied what could have been perceived as a marginal space as a gay, white male. He spent the 1970s being an activist for prisoners' rights, gay liberation, and the rights of psychiatric patients. My mother spent time in prison and was once a psychiatric patient—so this was familiar.

His Panopticon theory was audacious—I felt like Foucault wasn't a punk! He questioned why and exposed the truth. He shifted the focus from the individual to the power structure surrounding it. I enjoyed his word choice as he explained complexity and massaged his arguments. He also did not want his research to be published—another oddity about him that I liked. He died in 1984, the year I was born, so that always made me feel closer to him. Souls in passing.

I understood that as a critical theorist, the focus extends beyond mere discourse on domination and social realities for knowledge production. The goal, our goal, in the end, is to generate ideas that guide action to eradicate oppression. In my mind, this is why we are here!

My brain had space. I was preparing. I was ready. This crack baby. This monstrous baby. This member of the bio-underclass. This Black woman who is a Black daughter—of a Black mother, who was a victim of the crack cocaine epidemic and genocide.

This young, Black scholar was *doooooing* it honey. I moved forward. Minding my business. I didn't get what I always wanted in the coursework I received. That's cool. I didn't complain. I'm a doer. So, I just went out and got it. I was fortunate that I could walk across campus and find exactly what I was looking for in the Department of African American Studies to supplement what I was missing. At the time, I was interested in higher education policy, racial identity, and college student development. I was sitting in my proseminar class. My Professor was Dr. Molefi Asante. Because most Black students enrolled at Temple, who were also natives of Philly, knew of Dr. Asante as an elder and a prolific Black scholar, and educator. Everyone knew that Dr. Asante was the founder of *Afrocentricity* and established the first Ph.D. Program in African American Studies in 1988 at Temple.

We knew that Dr. Asante wrote the mandatory African American History curriculum for the Philadelphia School District. Philly was also home to a cluster of Afrocentric and African-centered charter schools that were heavily influenced by Asante and other African-centered intellectuals. I had the privilege of working at one of these schools for some time—*Imhotep Institute Charter High School.* Many of the elders, master teachers, and educators of these institutions also matriculated through the Urban Education program. These African-centered schools offered culturally relevant curriculum that incorporated African traditions and cultures. Black children across the city were learning about the Nguzo Saba and the virtues of Ma'at—it was critical pedagogy rooted in Black intellectual and cultural traditions. It was glorious. So, of course, I was his student—and learned all that I could because I recognized him as an elder, a master teacher—in theory and practice. In class, we were all working toward our culminating Master's theses, and I recall being extremely frustrated with the theoretical concepts of Vincent Tinto, a prominent educational theorist known for his research and writings on student retention and college success. While reading his theories, I found the gaps glaring, as they completely lacked any cultural context for diverse student populations. I was annoyed. The gaps—conjuring my side-eye.

Afrocentricity as a theoretical frame was a plausible alternative to me, and I could not understand why it was missing in nearly every College Student Development theory text. It just made sense! The way that I saw it, colleges and institutions of higher education were blatantly ignoring what was obvious in favor of Western and Eurocentric frameworks. I admit—that argument was a reach—but I was speculating and testing out my scholar-gangsta.

One day, I told Dr. Asante that I was really struggling with the literature in higher education, so much that I wanted to write a thesis debunking Vincent Tinto's theory altogether. Those were my words. I really believed that I could put pen to paper and write something so prolific that I could "debunk" one of the most influential and prominent educational theorists in the field.

The audacity!

Why wouldn't I think I could do this? I believed it was possible because, at any given time, I was reading *The Isis Papers: The Keys to the Colors* by Dr. Francis Cress Welsing for leisure. A Black woman carrying books in her purse like her aunties. Dr. Welsing was erudite and insightful. She once asked,

"Is it conceivable that a Black who is also a woman can critique and dismantle the whole of Western psychiatry?"

Then she proceeded to do so, so eloquent and effortlessly. I knew that she believed she could. A Black woman. A truth-teller. So why wouldn't I think the same? I got it from my elders—because ever since I was a girlchild, they told me to speak up, learn all that I could, so that I could become the smartest in the room. I believed them. So, that's what I did. As grad students, my peers and I were completely out of control—we were going to change the world! Young Black scholars on a mission. I was truly unhinged at the time—and I am grateful for my Professors who indulged me and my revolutionary critiques. So, I told Dr. Asante about my plan one day in class. He looked at me and said,

"Well, who's stopping you?

Do it, write it up, do the work, apply the method, and see what you come up with.

Write your critique and center Black students in their proper location!"

He'd go on to describe the dislocation of African people, particularly in education. To know Dr. Asante is to know that he is a master storyteller—it was the cadence of his speech and the gestures of his hands when he spoke. We always laughed at the hypocrisy! His classroom was our testimony; it was our meeting place. We left each week feeling inspired. He was right. No one was in my way. I understood my assignment clearly, and I had permission from my elder to proceed. I felt armored in this fight, so I went back to my advisors and shared my plan to critique Tinto's theory and Eurocentric frameworks in general in favor of an Afrocentric Model that could be used to explore and support college student development and retention of Black college students. The way that

I saw it, any framework that did not take into account the cultural and historical context of the subject under study was illogical.

The location of Black and Brown students was misplaced. Dislocated. I pulled Eurocentric frameworks out of their texts, placed them in my hand, and studied them. From my assessment, they were insufficient. Afrocentricity was a plausible solution, and I wanted to write through the arguments to make that case. I wanted to develop implications that policymakers could use to provide their students with programming and retention models that would set them up for success. That's really all that we educational scholars really want. To improve education in some way.

In my case, all that was required was the investment of resources and time, all of which colleges and institutions have allocated budgets for. I knew this to be true because I lived it. I worked full-time throughout grad school, and at one time, I was one of the youngest departmental administrators in the college I worked in, and my job was to manage the departmental budget alongside the Department Chair. Bridging theory and practice through policy was possible if there was buy-in. I digress.

By challenging Eurocentric frameworks, once again, I discovered not only the power of my own voice but also the transformative potential of embracing diverse perspectives. As I reflect on this chapter of my academic journey as an emerging Black woman scholar who dared to ask bold questions—I am reminded of the importance of questioning, challenging, and ultimately reimagining the dominant narratives that shape our understanding of education and society. So, I wrote a master's thesis challenging the philosophical foundation of higher education by exploring African and Eurocentric psychology and worldviews, arguing that African-centered frames were more appropriate for exploring the success, matriculation, and retention of Black students in higher education. It wasn't rocket science. I didn't even think it was creative or prolific. To me, it was just logical. It was the truth. I was simply using theory to tell the truth. In 2014, I became the first person in my immediate family to earn a Master's degree. That graduation was dope because Jill Scott earned her honorary Doctorate and was our commencement speaker. I looked up at her on that stage and was so proud. I did not view her as a celebrity at that moment. I viewed her as a big sister-cousin from around the way. Black women conferring degrees from Temple, in the same neighborhoods where we grew up.

While I was heavily influenced by bell hooks completing my Master's, I didn't *really* discover and engage Black womanist and feminist theory until I enrolled in my doctoral program. Immediate alignment. As a doc student, theory was still my love language. This is where I found my people. Young scholars in Philly convened, and we'd travel out west to University City to be in community with other scholars from around the city. It was there that I got to meet Dr. Kimberlé Crenshaw in 2015. She was the keynote speaker for the UPenn GSE Summit on Black Girls and Women in Education, which was sponsored by Penn's Center for the Study of Race and Equity in Education. Her presentation changed my life. She presented on *"Black Girls Matter: Pushed Out, Overpoliced and Underprotected,"* which was a national imperative to ensure the inclusion of Black girls and women in policy research, advocacy, and programmatic interventions. Say less. I left that summit ignited, and it was the point of no return for me. I would become a critical qualitative scholar dedicated to centering the voices of Black girls and women in educational research. I found my calling. So, I moved forward.

I remember my first time reading *"Black Feminist Thought"* by Dr. Patricia Hill Collins—that experience was nothing short of transformative. It took me a minute, but it was such a period of intellectual awakening and self-discovery for me. Each chapter of Collins' seminal work resonated deeply with me, affirming what I already knew and filling the gaps in my understanding of the complex history, politics, and perspectives of Black women. Our ways of knowing and our intersectional location were extensively written, well-researched—rigorous, analytical sound. Finally—I was reading our truth and seeing myself in the Black women scholars who used their mother's tongue to articulate our true location. Chapter eight, titled *"Black Women and Motherhood,"* always held a particular significance for me. Each time I revisited this chapter, it stirred something within me. A tingling. Goosebumps. It was page 196 that struck a chord, where Collins delves into the impact of the crack epidemic on Black women-centered networks in Bebe Moore Campbell's neighborhood. You see, this was not just any neighborhood. It was my neighborhood. Where my roots run deep. It was where my great-grandfather Otis owned a candy store in the 1960s over on Popular street and where my grandparents tended their garden next to the horse stables, cultivating fresh produce. Collins was speaking directly about my neighborhood, the place where my mother fell victim to the ravages of addiction and where my grandmother became my anchor and saved me. She said:

> The entire community structure of bloodmothers and othermothers is under assault in many inner-city neighborhoods, where the very fabric of African-American community life is being eroded by illegal drugs. But even in the most troubled communities, remnants of the othermother tradition endure. Bebe Moore Campbell's 1950s North Philadelphia neighborhood underwent some startling changes when crack cocaine flooded the streets in the 1980s. Increases in birth defects, child abuse, and parental neglect left many children without care. But some residents, such as Miss Nee, continue the othermother tradition. After raising her younger brothers and sisters and five children of her own, Miss Nee cares for three additional children whose families fell apart. Moreover, on any given night Miss Nee's house may be filled by up to a dozen children because she has a reputation for never turning away a needy child. (p. 196)

For anyone who has engaged with this particular section of Black Feminist Thought, I imagine that you may have read through it. Swallowing the brief acknowledgment of the crack era and maybe swiftly recalling a distant and weary experience triggering painful memories or physical aches within your body. I felt this too. But I also had some unexpected questions, like:

> *Okay - first of all, who is Miss Nee?*

> *What block did she live on?*

> *What hundred was it? Because I may have gone to school with some of her children.*

> *Did my people know Miss Nee?*

> *Is she still alive?*

> *How can I get in touch with Miss Nee?*

I didn't have to wonder too long because I knew of a few Miss Nee's on my block who were doing the same thing in the 90s when I was coming up. Page 196 became etched in my memory, the page adorned with highlights and circles, the top right corner folded down as a reminder. My *crumbtrail*. There was a longing there. A knowing that someday, I should return to it. I needed to because it felt incomplete. I knew this because I had lived it, experiencing firsthand the devastation wrought by the crack cocaine epidemic and genocide on Black women in my own family and community. Within the incompleteness lay an opportunity—a baton-pass. A chance to contribute my own narrative to bridge the gap between theory and lived experience. I envisioned weaving a personal essay alongside Collins' work, giving testimony, and asking for a witness. I imagined a call and response, affirming her arguments with my own truths. Adding a nuance to provide distinctions between what it was like for my grandma, whose daughter was lost—and how this pain was a different type of pain from the pain that my aunts experienced by losing a sister. Living in and through the crack epidemic changed us. I needed to write about it. What it meant for Black women. What it did to Black women and how it shaped Black girls born during and after the epidemic. This was a gap that I knew that I could fill someday. A gap that I couldn't fill before now.

Over the years, Black feminist and womanist theory became a touchstone in my explorations of Black women and girls in educational spaces. But I always found myself coming back to page 196. That page served as a necessary catalyst, guiding me to delve deeper, raise questions, speculate, and use my pain as fuel to expand upon existing theories. Page 196 was more than just a page in a book; it was a roadmap back to myself, and a roadmap towards a future where theory and lived experience converge to create a more inclusive understanding of Black feminist thought. I thought that maybe one day, someone could see my story on a page, triggering something bone-deep for them. A knowing that was always there. A knowing that was needed to continue the tradition of developing theory that shapes our lives.

After 40 years of living, I am ready.

Let Me Explain.

You're probably wondering—*Sis, how the hell did you come up with this?* Allow me to explain. The Sankofa Writing Method was birthed through an idea that came to me one night when I was journaling. A necessary download. I thought about how I could write my mother's counter-future to erase the violence she experienced throughout her life.

I am a social scientist, trained as an educational sociologist, with expertise in Black feminist epistemology and critical qualitative methodologies. As I explored my own trauma related to my mother's addiction, a new line of inquiry emerged, and I inevitably started looking at the social structures, systems, and institutions that influenced the crack cocaine epidemic and genocide.

Naturally, I was trying to conceive of a way that I could design some type of research study about exploring the experiences of people like me. The way that I saw it, our voices were completely removed from the conversation about the crack era in almost every public domain, publication, and modern documentary that I watched. A gap that is long overdue and needs to be filled. More specifically, I began deconstructing the *"Black Crack Mother"* stereotype as a controlling image. During all of this, I did what we scholars do and started asking questions. The first question was,

"Where are my people!?"

Because hunny, your girl was spiraling, and I just knew that I was not the only person going through this. I spent much of 2022 and 2023 asking myself bold questions. I wanted to understand how the children of parents who suffered from addiction navigated their educational pursuits. A.K.A—*How the hell did I end up with a Ph.D.?* I was particularly interested in exploring how the stigmas associated with the epidemic has (and still!) impacts Black women-centered networks. I wanted to (and will) write the remix of the generation after, who are now grown-ass individuals, professionals, and parents. I really want to know if life is "lifing" for them. More importantly, I wondered if I was the only fool on the planet subconsciously hiding pictures of their mothers or ancestors from their children. Was I the only person *rippin' and running* from this shadow? I was tired. And I yearned to be in a community with others like me. I always despised the term *"crack baby"* for the emotional triggers it creates. This language has us in a chokehold. These words have way too much power. Then, I remembered hermeneutics and the constructs we create through our language and our beliefs about words. So, I sought to study the crack epidemic beyond my lived experience. I sought to study the crack epidemic as a scholar. I sought out peer-reviewed articles, scoured every newspaper clipping, purchased every book published by academics and journalists. I read as much as I could and wrote as much as I could until I couldn't read and write anymore. This hurts. Writing through the historical context of the crack era was emotionally draining, triggering, and extremely difficult for me. Tears dripping. From a goddamn journal article. I wasn't only trying to make sense of a genocide that impacted Black communities all across the country, but I also started reexamining my own beliefs about my mother. It didn't help that almost everything that I read reproduced violence against Black bodies. This archive of historical data felt—incomplete.

Narrowing in on Black women, Black mothers, and Black daughters. That was a different type of pain.

Exhale.

You know the pain. It's a surge of emotion that boils over when we recall or even hear others describe the *unimaginable*. Renowned poet, activist, and scholar Dr. Sonia Sanchez wrote a poem about it once—*"For her Sister who took her child to a crack house, and left her child"* —the poem is called *"Poem for Some Women."* See, back in the day, we were watchers of Def Poetry Jam, and I remember being undone after listening to the mastery of this kind of storytelling. Only another Black woman truth-teller could capture the pain so eloquently. This was familiar because, as I said—I was a witness to my own mother's *nefarious activities*. The geeking. The freaking. I was born of it. Conceived by it. I didn't have to wonder—I knew it because I lived it. And I didn't want to discuss it. But I was finally able to critique it. I sought to see beyond the addiction and the pain.

I was searching for our mothers' humanity. Beyond the scholarship, most dominant media and popular culture imagery about Black women who were suffering from their addiction were mostly one-dimensional characters with very little depth—no backstory.

Bye Felicia—a colloquial phrase we still use. But what is Felicia's origin story?!

Exhale.

What happened to Felicia? These Black women and their *real* stories were missing. Their origin stories were missing. Erased. Their humanity was missing. I had questions.

Who would tell these stories, and when would "we" decide that it was time to tell them? Who would be the authors of these origin stories—of the ancestors who became ancestors too damn soon?

Much of what I read wreaked of the white gaze. Black people were misplaced. Dislocated. A discourse of mistruths buried in race-gendered oppression. It was mind-blowing. I needed to read something that restored Black women's humanity—Black people's humanity. Black scholars were also missing in action across disciplines on this topic.

Where were we?

Exhale.

I already knew that answer. The way that I saw it, we were *rippin' and running*. Writing about everything under the sun except this. Who *really* wants to talk about the crack epidemic and genocide? No one. It was too heavy a lift. It hurts, especially for those of us who lived it. I could barely discuss it myself, but I tried to examine the structures that shaped the dominant discourse surrounding it.

I discovered two books that resonated with me deeply on my healing journey. Books I would consider primers for those like me who choose to go deep and learn about the crack epidemic historically and sociologically beyond their lived experience. These are two extremely important texts synthesizing one of the least examined crises in American history from the perspectives of the individuals who were directly impacted. First, it was Dr. Tanya Telfair Sharpe, a Black woman truth-teller, senior behavioral health scientist, and epidemiologist at the Centers for Disease Control and Prevention, who wrote *Behind the Eight Ball: Sex for Crack Cocaine Exchange and Poor Black Women.*

Sharpe delves into the harrowing realities faced by marginalized Black women who engage in sex-for-drugs exchanges during the crack cocaine epidemic. Sharpe sheds light on crack abuse as a symptom of a larger societal problem, which is the disenfranchisement and neglect of poor Black Americans. She highlights the complex and often overlooked intersection of poverty, addiction, and survival strategies among marginalized communities. She also accurately locates the Black women in her research within their cultural, historical, and sociological contexts. She states,

> I view sex for crack and its consequences as empirical evidence of the multiple processes of long-term, consistent social exclusion and systemic racism that has worked to destroy poor Black American women's sense of self-identity. A fundamental part of this identity assault comes from gender roles for Black women developed in the context of slavery and segregation and based on erroneous concepts of Black inferiority and a complicated dual sexual image, both asexual and hypersexual at the same time. Another part of the assault comes from the structure of American economic opportunity, which often unrepentantly relegates Black women to the most basic roles. In addition, the wax and wane of the social policy toward Blacks opened short-lived windows of opportunity for the privileged few, closing quickly and ever defaulting to the same rhetoric expounding "black underservedness." (p. 3)

Through in-depth ethnographic interviews and analysis, Sharpe explores the psychological, social, and economic factors driving these sex-for-drugs exchanges, challenging dominant perceptions and highlighting the urgent need for comprehensive support and intervention measures. Sharp is a Black woman truth-teller—and her work brings the necessary attention to the systemic inequalities and vulnerabilities faced by Black women and Black women mothers suffering from their addiction and engaging in sex for crack exchanges. A necessary read.

Then, in the summer of 2023, Brother Donovan X. Ramsey, journalist, writer, and commentator, published *When Crack Was King: A People's History of a Misunderstood Era*. Donovan's work is powerful because of the narrative approach used to engage in conversations *with* those who were directly impacted. It was the voices of the individuals that were centered on their rightful position. Their voices amplified truth from divergent perspectives that humanized victims and key players who were there. People who *lived* it. Most importantly, Brother Ramsey *lived* it. He was not an outsider trying to make sense of what was happening to Black and Brown people in and around his own community, but he was writing *within* his lived experience, and his cultural understanding to try to make sense of what happened. He reflects as he states,

> Those who survived the crack epidemic, Black and brown people in particular, hardly ever talk about it. If we do, it's discussed wearily, like a trauma long accepted, in hushed voices and with thousand-yard stares. But we, survivors and second-generation survivors, want answers. We need to reconcile our memory and postmemory with all that we'd learned about the crack era in popular culture. We are piecing together fragments toward a real history. (p. 12)

Real history. While reading Ramsey's work, I realized that I was not alone. We were both second generation trauma survivors. I was relieved. Ramsey had the same types of questions and ponderings that I had.

Exhale.

Powerful and necessary reads. Purchase these books and pass them around to your friends and family at the next cookout. I was inspired, but nonetheless I was tired. I needed a break. So, the idea of re-writing my mother's liberation in a way that did not center the white gaze nor reproduce violence toward her body felt urgently necessary—because on some real shit, I realized that for me to *really* do this work, I had some more healing to do:

Real Shit

I needed a break from academic scholarship
I needed to write through my pain
I needed a safe space to shed these thug tears
Weary tears, from the depths of my soul
Tears for my inner girlchild
For the things that she's seen
Things no child should ever see
Tears for her yearning for her mother
Tears for the all the time stolen away
Tears for her wondering if she is worthy
Tears for her searching for mothers in others

Exhale

I needed a safe space to cry tears for my daughters
who will never get a chance to meet their maternal grandmother
For all the memories unmade
All the time stolen
For the implications buried in the questioning of 'Who their grandmother was'
For the warm embrace that only a grandmother can give
An embrace they will never know

Exhale

After my most ugly cries, I channeled the strength of my ancestors
Remembering to speak up
Reminding me who I am
This is so hard

Exhale

I wiped my tears, and I continued to write
Writing through the worlds I created for my mother in my mind
came easy like Sunday morning and I welcomed these thoughts with a

warm embrace
I marveled at the idea of 'writing her free'
I closed my eyes, and I imagined my mother resting well,
Laying easy, in a meadow or some flower field under a new sun
Smiling bright and unbothered
Hydrated. Calm. Imperturbable
Thique from good eatin'
Respite, peace, and joy was restored when I thought about my mother in this way. Using my radical imagination granted me access to a type of calm that I never knew that I possessed
So, I wrote like hell to capture the moments of my mind

Could you imagine this type of peace for your ancestors?

Exhale.

The way I saw it, there was no other person in my life, who deserved such rest
And as her daughter, I would be the one to give it to her

Creatively, I was unleashed!

I discovered an outlet
I wrote poems and not quite poems
And detailed memories, many of which centered my mother and many that did not
On my quest to find my mother's humanity, I suddenly recalled memories I had long forgotten…
Memories triggered the creation of new stories
Stories that erased the residue
What was this?

Exhale.

Phenomena was happening and I needed the language to describe it
I needed to know
I needed a framework

I needed a framework that serves us
I needed a framework that would allow me to resurrect hood tales and complicate epistemological, and ontological praxis in the same paragraph because I can and don't require anyone's permission to do so
I needed a framework that destroys the myth and amplifies the margin
I needed a framework that focused less on implications for policy and practice for institutions that never served us, and more on shit that I could actually use to heal this pain right now
I needed a framework that serves those of us who are secretly in need of healing from some form of cultural trauma. I needed a framework that allows me to combine theory with practice
Cuz' like Assata said, the two must go together
I needed a framework theoretically grounded in our knowing;
One that culturally centers us as agents because we are, and we don't have time to explain why
I needed a framework free from judgment and centered in my truth
I needed a framework that embraced my speculations and my musings
One that allowed me to write uninhibited
Easy
I needed a framework that gave me the space to process cultural trauma as a site for healing
I needed a framework that gave me practical tools
I needed a framework that embraced this energy
I needed a pathway

Exhale.

So, on the quest to search for my mother's humanity and to tell her story, I created one

I hope this answers the question of how the hell I got here. *"Real Shit"* originally started out as an audio I recorded. This was more of a spoken word, reflection to myself as I was describing why I needed to lean on theory and create a framework for the type of writing that was urgent for me. I titled that audio recording "Real Shit" because there was no academic equivalent. This raw response captures my process and is valid on its own. I began to reimagine my mother's existence, contemplating what her life could have been. This exercise was empowering; as I envisioned her liberation, I was envisioning my own. The act of documenting her imagined freedom became a form of resistance, empowering me to reclaim agency over her narrative and, by extension, my own. Through this process, I discovered unexpected sources of empowerment and resilience, underscoring the transformative potential of reimagining liberation. Black womanist and feminist epistemology taught me that the *process* of research is inextricably linked to the *product* of research. Once I knew that I wanted to write about my mother's futurity, I knew that I needed to map it. I needed a framework. I needed a method. I asked myself what it would take for me to do this. So, I started doing what I had always done since being a girlchild: I sought to theorize my way through. Like Polaris, I knew now that I was never alone. So, I gleaned into the truth-telling of Black women's theoretical and analytic prowess as my starting place. Because Black women were always truth-tellers and operators of my homeplace. From it all, I birthed a way of understanding my mother's counter-future through the lens of a speculative methodology. A framework and methodology that would allow me to *write her free.*

Exhale.

Towards An Endarkened Afrofuturist Feminist Epistemology & Shapeshifting in Qualitative Inquiry

In the forthcoming Routledge publication titled *Introduction to Afrofuturism: A Mixtape in Black Literature & Arts*, edited by Dr. DuEwa Frazier, I author a chapter titled *Quilting the Black-Eyed Pea: Exploring Endarkened Afrofuturist Feminism & Shapeshifting in Octavia E. Butler's "Wild Seed,"* where I introduce an *Endarkened Afrofuturist Feminist* epistemology, which is in conversation with two beautiful, brilliant and audacious Black Feminist Scholars, Dr. Cynthia B. Dilliard and Dr. Susana M. Morris. Dilliard reimagines *Endarkened Feminism* by questioning traditional feminist paradigms centered on white, Eurocentric viewpoints. Instead, she prioritizes the voices and wisdom of Black women and marginalized communities often overlooked in mainstream feminist discussions. She uses the term,

> *Endarkened* feminist epistemology to articulate how reality is known when based in the historical roots of Black feminist thought, embodying a distinguishable difference in cultural standpoint, located in the intersection overlap of the culturally constructed socializations of race, gender, and other identities and the historical and contemporary contexts of oppressions and resistance for African-American women. (p. 662)

Key aspects of an endarkened feminist positionality include the exploration of diverse cultural perspectives and knowledge systems, spiritual traditions as healing practices, recognizing the power of personal narrative and collective storytelling as sources of knowledge, resistance, and transformative education and pedagogy—fostering critical consciousness. Dillard also reminds us that we have been "seduced" as African ascendants into forgetting that we are mind, body, and spirit as African people. Dilliard's work enabled me, as a Black woman scholar, to explore endarkened feminism to articulate and acknowledge something that was already there—a way of knowing that captured my spirit and ethos as a scholar and educator. She once stated, "*It gives us a way to think ourselves together*" and "*To heal, we have to remember.*" Dillard emphasizes the power of (re)membering to move forward and the spiritual connection that propels us to move forward when the pain of remembering is too much.

Crunk Feminist Collective Co-founder and Black Feminist Afrofuturist scholar Dr. Susan M. Morris delves into the intersections of Black feminism and Afrofuturism, focusing on themes of power, identity, agency, and liberation for marginalized communities, particularly Black women. In *Black Girls Are From the Future: AfroFuturist Feminism in Octavia E. Butler's "Fledgling,"*

Morris coins *Afrofuturist Feminism* to consider the synthesis of Afrofuturism and Black feminist thought. She states,

> Afrofuturist feminism is a reflection of the shared central tenets of Afrofuturism and black feminist thought and reflects a literary tradition in which people of African descent and transgressive, feminist practices born of or from across the Afrodiaspora are key to a progressive future… just as Afrofuturism seeks to liberate the possibilities that open up when blackness is linked to futurity, so does black feminist thought seek to uncouple dominance from power as blacks assert their agency. (P. 153)

Endarkened Afrofuturist Feminism enables us to explore theoretical implications for using speculative modes to recover decolonizing technologies that can be employed for the success and liberation of Black women and girls navigating their present realities. I explore ways that we can both theorize and **take action** through the development of tools as a *praxis*—as in the application of theoretical concepts into practical actions and real-world settings for Black women and girls. I seek to deliberately integrate theory and practice—by engaging and experimenting with practical activities, modalities, interventions, and applications based on theory. Our business as scholars is about *doing* the work. As Dilliard so eloquently states,

> … An endarkened feminism seeks to resist and transform these social arrangements as well, seeking political and social change on behalf of the communities we represent as the purpose for research, versus solely the development of universal laws or theories for human behavior. (p. 678)

Through this work, I theorize my way through the scholarly discourse situated in Black feminisms, Afrocentricity, and Afrofuturist and speculative methods to develop freedom technologies that we can use to armor, protect, and heal ourselves.

Shapeshifting as a Freedom Device & Methodology

Shapeshifters
Black women can move mountains with a calculated glance
A whisper that will last generations
Exchanging ideas and sending telepathic messages to the other
Shapeshifters in the space
Playing coy as a disguise
Black women
Manifesting miracles with a wave of our hands
Snap, snap
Natural healers
Oracles
Operators
Always looking ahead
Assessing risks
Strategizing the next moves
We see through you
Check mate
Flowing through the chaos
Becoming hummingbirds to sit outside your windowsill and surveille the perimeter
Shapeshifting
A Black women's brilliance is unmatched
Of course, a Black woman wrote this book

Earlier, I mentioned that the *process* of research is inextricably linked to the *product* of research. The process by which I began thinking of an alternative future for my mother using the Sankofa Writing Method started from within—a process I refer to as *Shapeshifting*, which is a form of *Freedom Technology* and decolonizing speculative method of resistance that defuses any real or perceived threat to one's psychological and physiological state within any context.

In this work, *Shapeshifting* as a methodology implies flexibility, creativity, and agility in adapting to changing circumstances, problem-solving, or exploring diverse viewpoints.

Shapeshifting involves the deliberate use of spiritual consciousness, indigenous knowledge, and traditional wisdom, manifesting through intentional manipulation of one's body using creative and literal means as a form of resistance, self-definition, and survival. *Shapeshifting* is a defense mechanism, and I use this concept as an adaptation of a character named Anyanwu in Octavia Butler's *Wild Seed*. As the Black female protagonist, Anyanwu's character is an immortal, with the gift of healing herself and changing form into *any* animal or human. Anyanwu is *fierce*! She shapeshifts as a defensive mechanism whenever she needs to ensure her survival or to protect her kinfolk. As a daughter and a second-generation survivor of trauma, I have *Shapeshifted* my entire life, and I observed these same behaviors through the Black women who were raising me. *Shapeshifting*, for me, was demonstrated through this almost innate ability to heal myself. I recall many times when I felt extreme sadness, depression, anxiousness, and anxiety as a girlchild and as a second-generation survivor of trauma. My body absorbed it. There were moments when I actually wondered how I was able to act as if nothing was happening to me on the inside. Suppressing these emotions was part of the performance. The performance was a form of self-preservation to protect myself. I did not want, nor did I need anyone's empathy. I did not wear shame on my face and I did not want any handouts. I would earn respect through my ability to study and work hard. Mapping trajectories professionally and strategically positioning myself to be whatever it was that I needed to be. A Black woman's superpower—we morphed so that we could survive. *Black girl belonging* - we make ourselves belong. We do not wait until others or institutions make us feel welcome. We take our space. Operators of every homeplace.

Dr. Maya Angelou, prolific author, poet, and civil rights activist once stated *"The fact that the adult American Negro female emerges a formidable character is often met with amazement, distaste and even belligerence. It is seldom accepted as an inevitable outcome of the struggle won by survivors and deserves respect if not enthusiastic acceptance."*

Black women are brilliant by design and *Shapeshifting* is our gift. Genetic codes ensuring our survival. I engaged with this

Shapeshifting technology by becoming a chameleon whenever I needed to while navigating the social world, whether it be within educational spaces, or professional spaces. I use chameleon as a reference to the ways in which I morphed into a version of myself to blend in—using trickster technology; experimenting with versions of myself – making sure that I was always being judged by my merit and the integrity of my work and nothing more. Throughout my professional career, I was always *othered* by being *the only one*. The only Black person, or the only Black woman. It never phased me. I adapted quickly. I'm congenial, and I mastered the art of navigating challenging workplace relationships with my candor. I can initiate, facilitate and carry a conversation with anyone in the organization. People fascinated me—so I studied them, anticipating their needs. Just like my grandmother had always done. In almost every professional role, I was always the youngest—so *Shapeshifting* was not optional—it was a requirement. Ageism is real. I carried with me what it meant to occupy white spaces as a young person. It never helped that I truly have not aged since college. I do not say this to brag. Rather, I share this to articulate the challenges that I have had to navigate while occupying this body as a young Black woman in professional spaces. Being articulate at every turn and becoming an expert in every system, demonstrating my aptitude and my emotional competence to always be *on*. This is just what we do. I made it my business to learn my boss's jobs. To sit amongst leaders, studying them and their management styles. I became what I needed to become so that I could succeed. I grew up watching Black women *Shapeshift while taking no shit*. As I engage in this work of healing through cultural trauma, I also *Shapeshift* so that I may dig deep and excavate my mother's truths. The excavation process requires me to be a container. I needed to change form and create space so that I could unlearn and rebuild a space for my mother's possible future. This process required me to examine and explore every belief and truth stemming from my girlhood. The process required that I engage and relive traumatic events. *Shapeshifting* requires that we engage with our memories—from new vantage points, centering our ancestors as victims.

As a genre, Black speculative fiction and Afrofuturist conventions allow us to freedom dream and speculate through storytelling and writing as safe healing spaces. It enables us to employ the power of the written word to heal, express joy, and access imaginative maps that offer alternative truths and realities. As *Shapeshifters,* we can reimagine possible futures by applying freedom technologies to reimagine and reclaim ancestral narratives as a form of liberation. Through *Shapeshifting*, we can bend time and conjure back moments of pain, joy, desires, wishes, dreams, and pleasures of our ancestors as a decolonizing act. We do this through writing and mapping futurity through the timeless and unbounded realm of our imaginations. Rewriting ancestral stories allows us to speculate what could have been, what was, what is, and maybe—what *could be*! Writing is a political act. To write is an act of reclaiming what's ours, through the refusal of staying quiet about our oppression. Reclaiming ancestral stories is an open rejection of any other authority who has attempted to create a narrative of violence and subjugation for our ancestors. It is an open rejection of what has been considered a normative perspective of Black bodies through the white gaze. It is an open rejection of what has been considered neutral race claims of a pejorative other, Black people. It is an open rejection of any ontological and epistemological worldview and psychology that serves a racist agenda that functions to uphold a white supremacist structure. *Shapeshifting* not only enables us to rewrite stories of the past, but it allows us to rewrite our present and future in ways that do not recognize or pay any reverence to oppressive narratives created by authorities who sought to oppress us. As *Shapeshifters*, we conjure time. We choose when, where, and how we enter into the re(telling) of the narratives of our ancestors' stories. As a practice, we rewrite moments where joy was robbed from them. We do not recognize western divisions of time. There is only one time, which is now. This perspective allows us to bend and conflate time together as moments where we can center joy and healing for ourselves, and our ancestors as well. It's the reason why we come late to the cookout unless you want to be part of the set-up crew. What's understood doesn't need to be explained because it's Black secret technology. The convening starts when we are present and actively involved in the moment. This is where we agree. This is cultural. Tradition. We honor this culture through our writing. Time is when we say it is.

I engage in *Endarkened Afrofuturist Feminism* and *Shapeshifting* by weaving together memories and stories of my childhood as a self-healing, liberatory, and decolonizing literacy practice to (re) imagine counter-futures for my mother, one Black woman who was systemically disposed of during the crack cocaine epidemic and genocide. Some of us lost our mothers twice. I lost my mom long before my earliest memories of her. I never knew her in her natural state. I never knew her free, as a *Wildflower*. In my reflections as a daughter and as a scholar, I engaged in this work to "talk back" about an oppressive systemic experience that has and continues to affect me and my family. Through the process of *writing oneself free*, I bear witness to a new question:

What happens when Black daughters and Black daughter scholars begin to "talk back" for themselves and their mothers' future selves?

Daughter-Scholar Positionality Activated

I knew that I wanted to reimagine my mother's counter-future, but *how* I would write my mother's body was still a pondering for me. The idea of re-telling harmful occurrences and experiences my mother had just didn't sit right with me. I knew it to be true because I felt it in my body. I was troubled at the thought of divulging details about my mother's mental state. I didn't like the idea of describing the behaviors that made me uncomfortable because in doing so, I would be validating whatever emotion I felt while also invalidating my mother's truth, which was that she had very limited control of her behaviors due to her mental health state and the chronic conditions she suffered from. An oxymoron. Do you feel me? Maybe that was too many words. Let me try to simplify—I refused to write about my mother in a way that would bring her harm no matter how I felt about it. I knew what I was trying to do, but I was missing the language. I sought to resuscitate my mother and ask BOLD questions about her life. I was searching for a bridge and a way to map this idea qualitatively. I could not help it. I was searching for the language. I searched frantically through the scholarship—searching for myself in the data. Searching for myself in the eyes of the scholars I was reading. Something. Anything that could help me make sense of what I was conceiving of. I was questioning why I was even searching for validation within the scholarly discourse in the first place. I struggled with the genre I was bending for. I was annoyed because I really just wanted to write about my mother freely and tried to resist the urge to conform. I just wanted to write her future—but I was drained, and I was traumatized, and I didn't want to read anything else that inflicted harm on my mother's body.

Then, I heard my ancestors say,

"Chin up, baby girl. Speak up, baby girl. It's time."

I knew that I needed to do more. I needed to do the hard work. Writing my mother's counter-future was not enough. I needed to conceptualize what I was experiencing as a scholar. Rigorously. Scientifically. Theoretically. Methodologically. Analytically. So, I did.

I needed to do all of these things with a consideration of implications for policy and practice. And there it was folks—the *academic snapback*. I was trying my best to take a break. *I tried it.* Black women don't always recognize breaks. I needed to work through this ideation and exploration of phenomena so that I could massage the *hell* out of these arguments.

Then, I remembered my superpower, the one gifted to me by my *bloodmother* and my *othermothers*—I remembered that I just needed to *Shapeshift* so that I could become like water and flow through this qualitative process of recognizing myself as data. I would gather my feelings and put them in a Ziploc sandwich bag. Objectivity my ass. I sat them on a shelf for safekeeping. I needed to shake off my victimhood. I became clairvoyant like my grandmother, and I peered into the future. I realized the importance of avoiding triggers for trauma and steering clear of scholarly texts that could be harmful or emotionally taxing. To address this, I devised a risk mitigation plan that incorporated writing prompts and meditations. These tools would compel me to take necessary breaks and facilitate healing through my writing process. I would also read and apply the remedies and strategies offered in *Rest Is Resistance—A Manifesto* written by our good sister, lifesaving, a truth-telling Black woman—Tricia Hersey, creator of *The Nap Ministry*. Sending urgent messages to Black people all across this nation to put it all *on mute* so that we may rest!

I had a formula. I would write. Then, I would read. Then, I would rest. Repeat. Done.

I had a plan. So, I wiped my tears. Blew my nose. Took a shower. Brewed some tea. Then I got to work. I didn't get IRB approval for this *me-search*. My ancestors approved it.

I approved it. I did not need anyone else's permission to proceed.

Black Motherhood & Girlchildren

As a second generation trauma survivor, as a daughter-scholar of a mother who fell victim, and as a mother of two daughters, I engage in this work from a unique and intersectional perspective. As a Black mother, I show up in this work as a parent, acknowledging the importance of safeguarding my children at all costs. To achieve this, I deliberately use the terms "girlchild" and "girlchildren" to refer to myself as a child and to explicitly highlight my daughters' status as children, rejecting any attempts made to *adultify* them erroneously by prematurely imposing adult characteristics upon them due to their identity as little Black girls.

This distinction is crucial for me to operationalize. My colleagues and I address the prevalent and illogical implicit biases that leave Black girls vulnerable to violence within educational settings in our article, *Black Girls and Womyn Matter: Using Black Feminist Thought to Examine Violence and Erasure in Education*:

> The implicit biases against Black girls have also been well documented through attempts to adultify them erroneously. For example, according to research conducted by the *Georgetown Law Center on Poverty and Inequality*, Black girls are perceived as less innocent and more adultlike in comparison to their white peers between the ages of five to fourteen. The authors use the term adultification to generally describe a phenomenon which, despite established foundational moral and legal principles that protect children, effectively removes and reduces the consideration of childhood as a mediating factor in Black youths' behavior. (p. 36)

To counter these harmful perceptions, I intentionally refer to my daughters as "girlchildren," rejecting any notion that seeks to prematurely label them as angry or in need of harsh discipline. By using this term, I emphasize that their behavior should be viewed through the lens of childhood, necessitating patience and non-violent responses. Ultimately, my use of "girlchildren" is a deliberate choice to ensure that my daughters are not unfairly judged or misunderstood based solely on their intersectional identity as young Black girls, thereby positioning Black girls in their rightful context through language.

Long story short, *I don't play about my kids*!

Black Feminist–Womanist Storytelling & Critical Autoethnography

In this work, I draw from another brilliant Black woman scholar, Dr. April Baker-Bell, and *Black feminist–womanist storytelling* to re-write my lived experiences and that of my mothers. Informed by Black feminist/womanist epistemologies, Baker-Bell defines Black feminist—womanist storytelling as,

> A methodology that weaves together autoethnography, the African American female language and literacy tradition, Black feminist/womanist theories, and storytelling to create an approach that provides Black women with a method for collecting our stories, writing our stories, analyzing our stories, and theorizing our stories at the same time as healing from them. (p. 531)

Black feminist–womanist storytelling enabled me to reflect deeply and inform my method of writing through the selection of memories that I share (and choose not to share) and the creative process by which I engage in storytelling. Clearly, I was also writing a Black feminist critical autoethnography and gave a proverbial head nod to another dope Black woman scholar, who is also a Crunk Feminist Collective Co-founder by the name of Dr. Robin M. Boylorn.

Like Boylorn, I write, "*To make blackgirls visible, and through visibility to affirm them and (possibly) change their lives and worlds in the process.*" (p. 80) Through this work, I engage reflexive auto/ethnography as a conduit and bridge that connects the past with the future. Boylorn describes this as a form of "*doubled storytelling that moves from self to culture and back again.*" She states:

> ... Auto/ethnography values lived experience as data and allows researchers to be fully conscious as writers and participants in their narratives. Because it privileges the "I" and centers personal experience, auto/ethnography has the capacity to speak to/from both the margins and hyphens of subjective experiences. Engaging auto/ethnography as a way of making meaning and reimagining moments with new eyes and new insight introduces the possibilities of bridging (backward) in an effort to make sense and make meaning from difficult, painful, and complicated experiences. (p. 174)

I documented my process, and I engaged with my memories from new vantage points so that I could reinterpret them. Then, I used my writing as data to evaluate and measure the effectiveness of the Sankofa Writing Method to facilitate my own healing process. To really argue that my proposed framework was effective, I needed to validate it. So, I did.

I kept going. Like I always did. This time, at least, I was *rippin' and running* in the right direction.

Black women are truth-tellers, and it was Black women who modeled for me how to paint a portrait of my mother that would honor her dignity while also leaving space for me to process my pain. These Black women were scholarly oracles, disrupters, analytic assassins, and their methodological ponderings about Black people and Black women were incredible. Their names are Dr. Saidiya V. Hartman and Dr. Venus Evans-Winters. Their words were more than mere citations on a page to help strengthen an argument that I was trying to make. Their words, epistemological positioning, research questions, and scholarship were the antidote—herbal remedies for my *scholarsoul*. Their scholarship felt like something I could pull right up out of my great-aunt Julia's medicine cabinet. I am forever grateful to these Black women scholars—because they taught me how to write my mother's body in a way that honors her as an ancestor.

Critical Fabulation & Daughtering

It was Dr. Saidiya V. Hartman, scholar and cultural historian, and her concept of *"Critical Fabulation"* that completely blew my mind. Critical fabulation deals with the speculative reimagining of history to challenge dominant narratives and provide alternative perspectives. It is a writing method that seeks to displace authoritative accounts to reimagine what "could" have happened or what "might" have been said or done. Hartman developed a way of writing that challenges the limitations and omissions—she challenges the violence reproduced in historical archives—exploring themes of historical trauma, memory, and the complexities of Black female identity.

She challenges historical records by creatively reconstructing the lives and experiences of marginalized individuals, particularly Black women, who have been historically silenced. This method allows for the exploration of untold stories and the disruption of dominant narratives, contributing to a more nuanced understanding of the past and present. She was there all along, making a brief cameo in Jay-Z's prolific 4:44 video (appearing at minute mark 2:29), but I never knew that was her, and I didn't have the privilege yet to engage with her scholarship until now. It took me some time to find her. Then, finally, when I found her, I saw her—and then I saw myself. She looked like me, and it was the warmest embrace—and for the first time, I didn't feel crazy. I felt seen and even more proud to be able to extend and build upon such a beautiful genre and method of writing. Creating beautiful art created to fill the spaces and the voids.

I was enchanted and clung to Hartman's text. I studied her method of close narration in *Wayward Lives, Beautiful Experiments: Intimate Histories of Riotous Black Girls, Troublesome Women, and Queer Radicals*, and then I read her essay *Venus of the Two Acts*, where she examines and experiments with the violence of the Atlantic slave archive of a dead woman named Venus. In her attempt to redress what the archive omitted about Venus's life, Hartman tracks a process of writing *"At the limit of the unspeakable and the unknown"* to paint a more accurate picture of her life. Like Hartman, I aspired to tell a story about my mother without committing further violence in my own act of narration and storytelling. My goal in retelling my mother's counter-future resembled Hartman's contention with how Venus' life was written out. Hartman was *"Intent on achieving an impossible goal: redressing the violence that produced numbers, ciphers, and fragments of discourse, which is as close as we come to a biography of the captive and the enslaved"* (p. 3).

I smiled when she said, *"The intention here isn't anything as miraculous as recovering the lives of the enslaved or redeeming the dead, but rather laboring to paint as full a picture of the lives of the captives as possible."*

I smiled because my intention was quite the opposite. I wanted to be *audacious* and test my scholar gangsta—I wanted to *recover* and *redeem* the dead, my mother (our mothers), while also painting a more accurate picture of their lives. I believed that I could do both and I wanted to be explicit in my engagement with ancestral narratives. I wanted to trouble the concept of authority over my mother's story. As a daughter, I wanted to (and would) reclaim my mother's narrative so that I could critically trouble and complicate what was perceived to be her truth. I wasn't sure if this was miraculous or not—I guess we'll see. But at least now, I knew that if I could somehow combine this style of narration with speculative fiction conventions—then maybe I'd find a pathway to conceptually perceive my mother's futurity and methodologically ground the Sankofa Writing Method.

In this project, I also engage Black feminist scholar Dr. Venus Evans-Winters' concept of *Daughtering* to (re)imagine possible futures for my mother. Okay, Soror Dr. V snapped when she was writing *"Black Feminism in Qualitative Inquiry: A Mosaic for Writing Our Daughter's Body."* I threw the book across the room a few times. A masterpiece and a necessary read. She explains daughtering as a *"Tool of analysis in Black feminist qualitative inquiry is our own cultural and spiritual way of being, doing, and performing decolonizing work"* and as a process of *"Questioning, resisting, and deconstructing universal truth claims, grand narratives, and essentialism, while simultaneously, walking in and exposing our own contradictions."* Dr. Evans-Winters' work prepared me as a writer—teaching me how to approach the retelling of my mother's story while holding her in an extremely delicate place for me as a daughter-scholar.

She states,

> Daughtering invites an imagining of the possibilities of knowledge. How does engagement with inquiry and data service my family, my communities, my self-worth, and the person I want to become? How might knowledge of science help me become more humane, the world a safer and comfortable place, and help me understand the purpose of my life? What does a slice of culture, text, artifact represent

to my daughter, someone else's daughter, or a mother of a daughter or son? How can I help my analysis relate to the lived experience of a daughter? (p. 139)

Dr. Evans-Winters' work gave me permission to engage with my ponderings in a way that could directly benefit other Black women and girls as a decolonizing act for our healing and survival across social contexts. Dr. Evans-Winters' work helped me to protect and write my mother's body. I engage in *Daughtering* to pay homage to my mother's life and her counter-future. My silence in speaking about my mother has always been rooted in shame for what happened to her, to my family, and consequently—to me.

As a decolonizing practice, *Daughtering* enables me to look within while engaging in an ethics of love. From this position, I can develop tools that redefine perceptions of my mother's circumstances, erase the disruption of her past future selfhood, and re-write an imaginative liberatory future centering Black African and diasporic cultures through the creation of *Wildflowers*. Dr. V's scholarship provided the blueprint for how I was able to engage in this business of standing on the front lines for my mother. Beyond this exceptional methodological, truth-telling text, I was also a student of Dr. V's in her *Write Like A Scholar Bootcamp*.

Learning. Training. Studying. Preparing.

I was activated. These Black women armored me—and I would honor them in return through my scholarship and quest to continue the intellectual tradition of naming and defining our ways of being and knowing. As a scholar, *Daughtering* reminds me that I am never alone in the world. In the retelling of my mother's story, I reject attempts of voyeurism through the selective omission of traumatic events to keep *family business within the family and community*. In this light, daughtering as a process requires us to consider our kinship care responsibilities through the daughter scholar's ability to be *"Mindful of the memories we share orally or in writing for every time we speak, we may be inviting ancestors into not so sacred places"* (p. 139) Say that! Because real talk, there is a reason why it took me almost 40 years to tell this story.

There is a reason that most of us don't talk openly about our Black crack mothers and what it was like being daughters to them. It is us carrying forth the tradition. It's a practice of tradition that yields discernment on what information is shared with outsiders. Our practice of discernment is a form of protection. It not only protects me. But it also protects my mother, my grandmother, and the othermothers in my family who carried on the tradition of raising children born into our family. It is the reason that this story enacts *critical fabulation and daughtering* as I (re)write my mother's body. I don't share certain details about my mother *because, mind your business*. It is this selective omission that enacts my rejection of reproducing violence towards and against my mother's body through writing as a spiritual and sacred practice.

I was now able to conceptually, theoretically, and methodologically name my practice through the development of the Sankofa Writing Method.

Let's continue.

Chapter 2
Understanding The Sankofa Writing Method

There is no time for despair, no place for self-pity, no need for silence, no room for fear. We speak, we write, we do language. That is how civilizations heal.
~ Toni Morrison

So, What is The Sankofa Writing Method?

I developed the Sankofa Writing Method, drawing inspiration from the works of bell hooks. In *Teaching to Transgress: Education as The Practice of Freedom,* hooks celebrates the radical possibilities of educational spaces that allow for teaching practices that encourage transgression as a movement against and beyond boundaries. Similarly, the Sankofa Writing Method is a five-step framework that situates writing as a practice of freedom and healing spaces where we can push beyond the boundaries of our imaginations by remembering, recovering, and moving forward toward our liberation.

Key characteristics of the Sankofa Writing Method include leaving everything on the page, deconstructing dominant narratives, connecting emotions to events, and reclaiming agency and power through storytelling. This immersive process helps us piece ourselves back together, retaining authorship over our lives. The etymology, or the meaning of the word "Transgress" means to "Step across or beyond." This is why we are here. We are here to write ourselves free by *crossing over, to, through, and beyond* our trauma, our deepest fears, and our shame. Writing to transgress means that you are ready to prioritize your mental health and acknowledge your trauma. Sis, if you are Black, alive and well, and reading this book, you are traumatized. We all are. However, if you're reading *this* book, it's because you, or someone you know, has experienced a specific type of cultural trauma or trauma directly connected to the crack cocaine epidemic and genocide.

Recognizing and naming this is important because our trauma is rooted and buried under a complex web of pathologies and stereotypes that were created and designed to root our subjugation. In my own healing journey, I found that many of my beliefs were constructed through the lens of societal portrayals and discourses about my mother. Such portrayals and discourses are distortions. Myths. Lies. Garbage. Once I set intentions to recover my mother's truth, I recognized that these portrayals did not serve me. So, I created a new lens. One that would allow me to see my mother for what she was—to see her truth.

Selecting the name for this method came intuitively to me. The term *Sankofa* is a West African word with origins from the Akan tribe in Ghana, which translates to "To go back and fetch it," symbolizing the importance of remembering and obtaining knowledge from your past in order to move forward. The interpretation used within this method amplifies the significance of our quest for knowledge, remembering that our pasts must never be forgotten. To move toward a progressive future, we must know where we come from. This practice and this tradition have been indicative of our survival.

The Sankofa Writing Method is a form of freedom technology, which are tools used to resist oppressive conditions that enable us to survive our present realities. It is a transgressive and transformative tool for coping with and navigating cultural trauma through storytelling while reclaiming ancestral narratives. This method allows us to write through our pain and explore our own judgments and biases. Through this method, we deconstruct our narratives and examine our histories, all while healing and imagining new possibilities and counter-futures for our loved ones. Through this method, I document how I rewrite pieces of my mother's narrative, reimagining her as a *Wildflower*—a free spirit. By definition, *Wildflowers* are unbothered, and they grow naturally and freely in the wild, blooming in natural landscapes like meadows and forests without any human intervention or cultivation.

Metaphorically, the term *"Wildflower"* describes someone who is independent, and unbounded by societal norms and expectations. In the realm of personal development, healing, and writing futurity for my mother, rewriting her life as a *Wildflower* is a deliberate disruption and counter to the violence she endured. (Re)imaging and rewriting her freedom is a deliberate rejection of the stereotypes that were constructed about her through societal ideologies associated with race, gender, and class oppression. Re-writing my mother as a *Wildflower* restores her uniqueness, her truths, and her ability to thrive without adversity.

Cultural Trauma & Restoring Black Family Structures

In this work, cultural trauma refers to the collective psychological distress experienced by members of a community or society because of a significant and distressing event or series of events that have a profound effect on their identity, values, beliefs, and sense of belonging. Examples of traumatic events include genocide, colonization, forced displacement, natural disasters, war, or other forms of systematic oppression and violence. Cultural trauma often leaves a lasting impact on the collective narratives and memory of a community. At the core of this writing method is a direct focus on healing and repairing the Black familial structure. In this work by developing curriculum, I draw from prominent sociologist and scholar of African American Studies, Dr. Clovis Semmes, and his articulation of Black cultural trauma and the necessity to consider the histories of Black survival and the implications this has for the Black family structure. In his article *Foundations of an Afrocentric social science: Implications for curriculum-building, theory, and research in black studies*, he states:

> One example of a category of analysis linked to the cultural trauma arising from contact with Europe in the fifteenth century is the disruption of the Afrikan family. We know that the family is primary in generating, preserving, and transmitting culture. Thus someone interested in Afrikan cultural regeneration would want to know how to build-strong family structures which are functional to the survival and prosperity of Black people. In addition, the basis of historical comparison and analysis is traditional Afrikan family life and not European family life. One's concern should not be whether or not Black family structures approximate white family structures, but whether their present forms are useful to the needs of Black people. Thus, the study of the Black family is a legitimate concern of Black Studies, but only when understood from the perspective of its relevance to the survival and prosperity of Black people and not as a social problem for the white community. (p. 9)

The Sankofa Writing Method as a curriculum is a decolonizing tool—a freedom device developed to serve the needs of Black people through the preservation of our bloodlines.

Grounding Our Writing Practice Using Black Speculative & Afrofuturist Elements

The Sankofa Writing Method embraces Black speculative fiction as a tool to perceive Black futurity. Black speculative fiction is a type of literature that explores alternative histories and possible futures. Afrofuturist literature is commonly categorized within speculative fiction, as it regularly integrates aspects of science fiction, fantasy, and speculative themes into its stories. Afrofuturism sets itself apart by prioritizing Black experiences, cultures, and histories in its depictions of the future. Afrofuturism expresses notions of Black identity, agency, and freedom through art, creative works, and activism that promote liberated Black futures.

In *Afrocentricity in Afrofuturism: Toward Afrocentric Futurism*, Smith and Asante argue that for Afrofuturism to progress with a strong Pan-African purpose, the Afrocentric approach must be used to examine the possibilities of Black futures. In this work, I agree that an Afrocentric framework must be rooted in the process of excavating our cultural trauma and perceiving Black futurity. Also, while exploring speculative and literary texts and developing decolonizing methodologies for educational research, S.R. Toliver expands upon prior Afrofuturism definitions in her book *Recovering Black Storytelling in Qualitative Research: Endarkened Storywork*. She defines Afrofuturism as a cultural aesthetic where Black authors craft speculative narratives centering on Black characters to reclaim the past, counter negative realities, and envision new futures. Toliver suggests framing Afrofuturism as an aesthetic as a way to offer a flexible approach to capture various stylistic elements found in speculative texts, and in this work, I view Afrofuturism as an aesthetic that offers a portal to create and imagine futures that inspire healing and hope in Black communities. This framing allows us to freedom dream and speculate through storytelling and writing as a safe space. It enables us to employ the power of the written word to heal, express joy, and access imaginative maps that offer alternative truths and realities.

The Sankofa Writing Method Toolkit

While perceiving futurity, it is important to allow your radical imagination to run free, so I have designed the Sankofa Writing Method toolkit to inspire and spark creative ideation for your writing as a sacred practice. Below are a few examples of ways to incorporate Black speculative and Afrofuturist conventions through your writing and storytelling:

- ❖ Literary Restoration: Through our writing as a sacred practice, we safeguard the legacy of our ancestors and transcend the white gaze by focusing on reclaiming their narratives. This sacred endeavor prohibits the perpetuation of harm and the infliction of violence or stress upon our ancestors' bodies through our storytelling, whether written or spoken. Engaging in this intentional practice is a tribute to honor and show reverence to our ancestors.

❖ Empowering Marginalized Voices: Afrofuturism amplifies marginalized voices, providing a platform to share our own stories on our own terms. By centering the experiences and perspectives of Black characters, Afrofuturist writing challenges dominant narratives and celebrates diversity.

❖ Bending Time: This method of writing does not conform to Western and Eurocentric perceptions of time. Chronology is an illusion. Through *Sankofa*, we bend time and untie the years. We go backward, forward, upward, and downward. We wrap our arms around future generations. We occupy four-dimensional space. Time is malleable, circular, cyclical, and synchronous—which stimulates creative and imaginative possible futures. Time is agreed upon through our communion—and our collective agreement.

❖ Speculative Futures: Through an Afrofuturist lens, we can envision future societies where Black people play central and empowered roles as agents. This can involve imagining advanced civilizations built upon Afrocentric principles, exploring themes of innovation and liberation.

❖ Centering African Mythology and Folklore: Afrofuturist writing often draws inspiration from African mythology and folklore—weaving together ancient stories, tales, songs, and legends into futuristic narratives. By incorporating elements of traditional African spirituality and cosmology, we can reimagine nuanced worlds for our ancestors that center and honor Black cultural traditions.

❖ Critiquing Power Structures: Using a speculative lens provides a platform for critiquing contemporary power structures and systemic injustices. As writers, we can use speculative fiction to explore themes of oppression, resistance, and social change, offering alternative visions of justice and liberation.

❖ Exploring Technology and Innovation: Afrofuturism embraces technology as a tool for empowerment and

liberation. Writers can explore scientific technologies, and innovative digital cultures within their narratives, imagining how these developments intersect with African and Black diasporic experiences.
- ❖ Lastly, do you! These are broad concepts on ways that you can creatively apply the method through writing as an art form. The boundaries are limitless, so use this time to really stretch your imagination and let your radical mind run free.

The Framework

The Sankofa Writing Method offers a five-step framework for healing from cultural trauma:

1. Remember to Talk Back
2. Excavate Trauma
3. Destroy the Myth
4. Amplify the Margin
5. Go Free, Wildflower

Remembering to Talk Back is about finding your voice, confronting your shadows, and deconstructing your beliefs. This step requires us to actively seek out knowledge so that we can speak up assertively to challenge norms, and systemic oppression.

Excavating Trauma requires us to dig deep and take inventory of our memories so that we can unravel the roots of our histories and engage our deepest fears and our shame head-on. Through this process of excavation, we peel back the layers of intergenerational trauma, societal injustices, and historical legacies that have shaped our experiences. By identifying *critical traumatic events*, we lay the groundwork for healing and eventual reconstruction of ourselves and our stories.

Destroying the Myth is about our insistence to lift the veil and stay as close to our ancestors' truth as possible by centering them as victims and challenging dominant worldviews and perspectives about them. Through self-definition, recovering ancestral truth refers to the process of rediscovering and reclaiming authentic narratives and experiences that may have been obscured or suppressed by external influences, societal norms, or personal trauma. This step requires you to set aside your feelings and seek knowledge so that you can challenge your beliefs.

Amplifying the Margin deals with finding the silver lining—and recognizing the beauty that resides in marginal spaces through the rich cultural tradition of Black families and Black women-centered networks nurturing and caring for one another as a sacred and cultural practice. Amplifying the margin is about cherishing and capturing moments when our ancestors experienced being cared for, joy, pleasure, and love as empowering and validating experiences.

Go free, Wildflower captures the final culminating step where we liberate our ancestors. In this step, we integrate all that we've learned through our journey to creatively write our liberation, drawing from Black speculative and Afrofuturist conventions. In this step, we *write our ancestors free.*

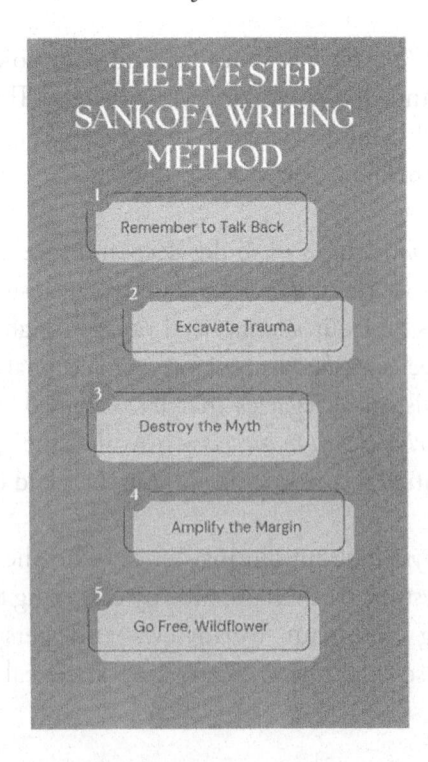

THE FIVE STEP SANKOFA WRITING METHOD

1. Remember to Talk Back
2. Excavate Trauma
3. Destroy the Myth
4. Amplify the Margin
5. Go Free, Wildflower

Healing Through *Nommo* & Storytelling

As part of the conception of the Sankofa Writing Method, I engage *Afrocentricity* and *Nommo* to intentionally glean into the Black lexicon, communication sensibilities, and oratorical experiences rooted in traditional African philosophies—channeling the history of storytelling of our ancestors and the oral traditions of Black people. *Nommo* is an African-centered word that represents the creative power of the spoken word to generate and create reality. *Nommo* brings about harmony, balance, and transcendence within and across a rhetorical space. The process of re-writing my mother's story as a *Wildflower* signals the regeneration of her story as a life force through the creation of an alternative reality. A disruption. Engaging in *Nommo* enables me to also engage with my mother as an ancestor. Through the Sankofa Writing Method, I utilize characteristics of *Nommo* to reconstruct Black diasporic cultures' community and cultural experiences through narrative. In this way, I believe that the creative power of the spoken word as it is passed down through traditions, values, and memories also transcends to the written word through the retelling of our ancestors' stories.

Next, you must realize there is healing power in the spoken and the written word. Reclaiming our narratives through writing and storytelling has a number of benefits. Research shows that expressive writing is a tool for healing and lowers blood pressure, strengthens our immune systems, and improves overall physical and psychological well-being. Writing is therapeutic and allows us to slow down and reflect on our feelings so that we can improve our self-awareness. Writing also allows us to cope with complex emotions while gaining clarity and identifying solutions. Below are a few additional benefits of storytelling:

- ❖ Empowerment: Sharing one's story allows us to take ownership of our experiences and assert our agency. By telling our own stories, we can reclaim our power and resist being defined solely by our trauma.
- ❖ Validation: Storytelling provides a platform for us to validate our own experiences and feelings. Through storytelling, we

can affirm the validity of our emotions and perspectives, which is essential for healing.
- ❖ Catharsis: Sharing one's story can be cathartic and emotionally freeing. It provides an opportunity to release pent-up emotions, traumas, and burdens that may have been internalized for years.
- ❖ Connection: Storytelling fosters connection and community. By sharing our experiences, we can find validation, empathy, and support from others who may have had similar experiences. This sense of connection reduces feelings of isolation and fosters a sense of belonging.

Overall, reclaiming one's narrative through storytelling is important because it provides a platform for empowerment, validation, catharsis, connection, reframing, and integration—all of which are essential components of the healing process.

Naming Our Cultural Trauma

We all have trauma. Mine is directly connected to my mother's addiction stemming from the crack cocaine epidemic and genocide, which was chemical and biological warfare waged against Black communities across the United States between 1980-1995. The crack epidemic had widespread social consequences on families and communities. Some of the widespread effects include the following:

- ❖ Breakdown of Families: The epidemic contributed to the destabilization of families as addiction tore apart households, leading to increased rates of separation, divorce, and single-parent households.
- ❖ Child Welfare Issues: Many children were left neglected or abandoned due to parental addiction, resulting in higher rates of children being placed in foster care or raised by grandparents or other relatives.
- ❖ Increased Crime and Violence: The rise in crack cocaine use fueled a surge in crime and violence in affected communities, leading to higher rates of homicide,

robbery, and other crimes.
- ❖ Health Problems: Substance abuse related to crack cocaine led to a host of health issues, including addiction, overdose deaths, and the spread of diseases such as HIV/AIDS due to needle sharing among users.
- ❖ Economic Disparities: The crack epidemic disproportionately affected low-income communities, exacerbating existing economic disparities and perpetuating cycles of poverty.
- ❖ Stigmatization and Discrimination: Communities impacted by the crack epidemic often faced stigmatization and discrimination, both from within and outside their communities, further marginalizing already vulnerable populations.
- ❖ Incarceration Rates: The "War on Drugs" policies implemented in response to the crack epidemic led to a surge in incarceration rates, particularly among Black and Latino populations, contributing to the phenomenon of mass incarceration and its associated social and economic consequences.
- ❖ Psychological Trauma: Individuals and families affected by the crack epidemic experienced significant psychological trauma, including stress, anxiety, and depression, which further strained community resources and support networks.

Why is this important?

Recognizing trauma, particularly for Black women, is crucial due to the significant health consequences associated with trauma-related stress. Traumatic experiences, often stemming from childhood, include exposure to violence, mental illness, substance abuse, abuse, and neglect, leading to various physical and mental health issues such as shame, anxiety, depression, higher rates of suicide, heart disease, and substance use disorders.

Black women are disproportionately affected by intergenerational trauma, transmitted through generations, which impacts our health and affects familial relationships and parenting practices within Black communities. Race-gendered trauma resulting from systemic racism exacerbates mental health challenges like depression, anxiety, and PTSD among Black women. High rates of cardiovascular diseases and maternal mortality further highlight the health disparities faced by Black women. Generally, Black communities in the United States have experienced immeasurable rates of complex trauma for generations, and research has consistently shown that Black individuals experience higher levels of trauma-related stress than any other demographic, which is compounded by the impact of historical, race-based oppression across generations. The first step in the journey toward healing is to be deliberate in naming our trauma. Ignorance and excuses are tools of the incompetent, and as Black women, we cannot afford to be fools. So, ask yourself:

Do I want to recover and heal from my trauma?

Am I willing and ready to do what needs to be done?

Am I ready to think critically about my ancestors and their circumstances?

I believe that you are ready. You can do this, and I will guide you along the way.

Applying The Sankofa Writing Method

Affirmation
I release feelings of shame around my identity

Putting Concepts into Action
Now, it's time to translate concepts into tangible actions. It's important to prioritize your mental health needs, and this looks different for everyone. Below are examples of practices you can adopt in your healing journey:

- ❖ Self-Care: Dedicate "you-time" to activities that promote relaxation and reduce stress, such as exercise, meditation, scheduling a massage *because you deserve it*, yoga, or other hobbies.
- ❖ Seek Support: Reach out to friends, family members, or mental health professionals for emotional support and guidance when needed. For some, connecting with a licensed professional with shared cultural experiences is essential for establishing a meaningful connection to explore cultural trauma. This was a requirement for me. This process can be cathartic for some individuals while triggering for others. Seeking support from a professional clinician is always a wise decision.
- ❖ Practice Mindfulness: Engage in mindfulness techniques to stay present and manage overwhelming thoughts or emotions effectively.
- ❖ Setting Boundaries: Set boundaries within your networks to help safeguard your personal space, time, and resources. Protecting your peace during this journey allows you to stay focused on your healing while prioritizing self-care, hobbies, and responsibilities without feeling obligated to constantly meet others' demands. I completely fell off the grid as I was going through my healing journey. Channeling Beyonce—I'm talking, *look around, everybody on mute*. This happened naturally as I was preserving my energy for my writing practice.

Writing Prompts

- ❖ Reflect on your sources of trauma and consider how resolving them could positively impact your life. Use your audio recorder app or journaling as a tool to document your responses.
- ❖ How do you currently prioritize self-care in your daily life? Are there any additional self-care practices you'd like to incorporate?
- ❖ Reflect on your sources of trauma from childhood or

observations of trauma, whether indirect or direct. Describe these experiences in detail, including how they have affected you.
❖ Explore the emotional and psychological effects of your trauma. Write about any patterns or behaviors that have emerged as a result and how they have influenced your life.
❖ Imagine a future where you have healed from your trauma. Describe what this future looks like and how it differs from your current circumstances.

Chapter 3
Remember to Talk Back

Moving from silence into speech is for the oppressed, the colonized, the exploited, and...it is that act of speech, of "talking back" that is no mere gesture of empty words, that is the expression of moving from object to subject, that is the liberated voice.
~ bell hooks

The first step in the Sankofa Writing Method is about remembering to *talk back*. Remembering to *talk back* is about finding your voice, confronting your shadows, and deconstructing your beliefs. In *Talking Back: Thinking Feminist, Thinking Black*, bell hooks talks about writing as a way to capture speech, to hold onto it, and to keep it close. She also talks about speaking as more than just an expression of creative power but as an act of resistance that challenges dominant power structures that render Black women nameless and voiceless. The concept of "talking back" is a way to encourage marginalized individuals, particularly women and people of color, to engage in dialogue and challenge dominant narratives or power structures. "Talking back" is a defiant act of challenging norms, systemic oppression and asserting our power through speaking up, asserting our agency, creating counter-narratives— that address misrepresentations. Moving from silence into speech is an audacious act, and it is precisely what we are here to do.

To articulate your story, you must take ownership of your story because it is yours. It doesn't belong to anyone else. This work is about moving ourselves from the margins to the center. This work is about being loud about what transpired, dissecting it, putting the pieces back together, breaking them apart, and putting them back together again. We must examine our beliefs so that we can become empowered to articulate our truth. We must go beyond looking back to wonder. Finding our voice requires us to channel *Sankofa* so that we may look back and gain the knowledge needed to move forward.

Confronting Your Shadow

Going back requires us to look within. In our healing journey, confronting our truth, or what Swiss psychiatrist Carl Jung calls our "Shadow," is pivotal. The Shadow represents the parts of ourselves that we keep hidden or suppressed, often stemming from traits we're not proud of or emotions we find uncomfortable. By avoiding these aspects of ourselves, we risk projecting our issues onto others or experiencing triggers that disrupt our peace. Engaging in shadow work entails delving into these suppressed aspects of ourselves, bringing them into conscious awareness, and integrating them into our identity. To identify your shadow, reflect on what triggers you and your emotional responses. Consider the parts of yourself you reject or hide due to embarrassment or fear of judgment. Anything that threatens how you present yourself to the world likely resides in your shadow. The goal of this work is to understand and integrate these aspects into our identity to achieve balance, harmony, and authenticity in our healing journey. Shadow work is also a way for us to continue the tradition, as the concepts of polarity, balance and harmony are all deeply rooted in Indigenous and African spiritual traditions that recognize the interconnectedness of all things, including the seen and unseen, the conscious and unconscious. From this perspective, the shadow represents an individual aspect of our psyche and is the source of imbalance—oftentimes rooted in our trauma. In my own journey, confronting my shadow involved deep self-reflection on my childhood, my mother's addiction, and my beliefs about her. Deconstructing these beliefs allowed for greater self-awareness, emotional healing, and personal growth. Engaging in shadow work can be done alone or with the guidance of a licensed therapist, spiritual teacher, or healer. The method you choose is personal, but having professional support can provide valuable guidance and insight throughout the process.

Deconstructing Beliefs

Getting to the root of my own beliefs about myself and my mother forced me to see the truth. The truth is that while I was accepting and understanding about my mother's addiction, I was still thinking about her through a societal lens that reproduced negative stereotypes about her and subconsciously made me feel ashamed. Also, I was aware that the "crack baby" myth was not real; however, the residue of the "crack baby" and "crack mother" stereotypes were etched so deep into my psyche that I found it almost impossible to separate the myth from the truth. I was constantly proving to myself that I could do anything I set my intentions on. I didn't want to be associated with the crack epidemic, and I didn't want any negative associations to define me.

Understanding this as my shadow, I knew that I needed to explore internalized beliefs about my mother, her addiction, and Black motherhood during the crack cocaine epidemic and genocide. To see my mother's truth, I needed to *Shapeshift* so that I could become a container—so that I could leave space to unlearn and separate fact from fiction. I needed to be informed so that I could define the source of my beliefs. I needed to enact Sankofa by going back to fetch the truth so that I could bring it forward. I needed to explore the reason why the pathology of these "crack mother" and "crack baby" labels were triggers for me and others like me. What I discovered was that despite more than 20 years of scientific and medical research debunking the myth of the crack baby, along with apologies from media outlets, the sheer extent of misinformation perpetuated by the media, political rhetoric, irresponsible journalism, and the reinforcement of negative imagery and stereotypes was so massively overwhelming within popular culture and the public and political discourse, that the damage of the myths was already implanted—penetrating the very fabric of how society views Black people suffering from addiction. Attempts to debunk the myths have been completely inadequate and insufficient compared to the sensationalism and frenzy created by the media in the first place. To move forward in this healing journey toward achieving a liberated voice, I needed to fetch the knowledge required to situate my mother as the subject to see her truth clearly. Class is in session. The following sections in this chapter provide a bit of historical context about the crack era, associated myths, and the role of Black women who were victimized.

Recognizing Controlling Images and Stereotypes

Before we go forward, it is important that we have the language and information to name our oppression and that of our mothers. We must examine controlling images and stereotypical tropes that have shaped societal attitudes toward Black women. Controlling images, particularly in the context of critical race theory and Black feminist theory, refer to stereotypical representations or portrayals that shape societal attitudes of marginalized groups that serve to reinforce existing power dynamics and justify oppression. These images are designed and perpetuated through various forms of media, literature, and cultural narratives, influencing how Black women are perceived and treated in society. A trope is defined as a commonly recurring theme or device in literature, media, and other forms of storytelling to convey emotions and ideas. In *Black Feminist Thought: Knowledge, Consciousness, and the Politics of Empowerment*, Sociologist Dr. Patricia Hill Collins highlights the following examples of controlling images and stereotypes about Black women:

- ❖ The Jezebel: Portrayed as sexually promiscuous, hypersexualized, and morally loose, the Jezebel stereotype depicts Black women as seductive and sexually available, reinforcing harmful notions of Black female hypersexuality.
- ❖ The Mammy: Derived from the stereotype of the enslaved Black woman as a caretaker and nurturer, the Mammy stereotype portrays Black women as selfless, submissive, and

obedient maternal figures, often depicted as overweight, asexual, and devoted to serving white families.

- ❖ The Sapphire: Also known as the "Angry Black woman" stereotype, the Sapphire portrays Black women as loud, aggressive, confrontational, and emasculating, perpetuating the idea that Black women are inherently hostile and difficult to deal with.
- ❖ The Strong Black Woman: While seemingly positive, the Strong Black Woman stereotype places unrealistic expectations on Black women to be resilient, self-sacrificing, and emotionally invulnerable, ignoring their humanity and vulnerability.
- ❖ The Welfare Queen: Rooted in racialized stereotypes of poverty and welfare dependency, the Welfare Queen stereotype portrays Black women as lazy, irresponsible, and exploiting the welfare system for personal gain, perpetuating stereotypes of Black women as dependent and undeserving.

Similarly, the depiction of Black crack mothers as the "Bad Crack Mother" icon perpetuates yet another "controlling image" and trope, portraying Black women as bad Black mothers and deviant figures within political discourse and pathologizing them as primary targets within Black communities. Scholarly research has delved into the impact of misrepresentations about Black crack mothers in various forms of media, including film, music, and literature, shedding light on how these portrayals have influenced oppressive legislation and policies that disproportionately punish poor women of color, thereby cementing the image of the Crack Mother in mainstream consciousness. Such images reinforce systemic inequalities and biases, influencing how Black women are perceived, treated, and represented in various aspects of society. These depictions contributed to the criminalization and demonization of individuals, particularly women of color, who were struggling with their addiction and often facing socio-economic challenges. Recognizing and challenging these stereotypes is essential for situating our ancestors. Are you with me?

Let's continue.

Deconstructing the Crack Mother Icon and Crack Baby Myth

Deconstructing the Black crack mother trope connects to the debunking of the crack baby myth. In *Killing The Black Body: Race, Reproduction, and The Meaning of Liberty*, another Black woman, a truth-teller and legal scholar, Dr. Dorothy Roberts, delves into the complex intersection of gender, race, and reproductive rights for Black women in the United States. Roberts questions the selective focus on crack cocaine in prosecuting maternal behaviors, arguing that other substances and activities pose equal or significantly greater risks to fetal development, including drinking alcohol, drinking coffee, smoking cigarettes, prescription and nonprescription drugs, etc. In fact, prenatal alcohol exposure is the most commonly known cause of intellectual disability in this county, and cigarette smoking has been statistically linked to spontaneous abortion and sudden infant death.

Contrary to common belief, crack cocaine use *does not* correlate with the severity of these defects. The exaggerated media-driven myth of the crack mother and crack baby refers to the widespread belief that mothers who used crack cocaine during pregnancy would give birth to severely disabled and dysfunctional children known as "crack babies." It was the powerful imagery of tiny babies who were severely disabled and dysfunctional, which were used to justify the criminalization of Black mothers, turning drug use into a crime. This myth contributed to the stigmatization of Black women, portraying them as irresponsible and unfit mothers. Media hysteria fueled societal panic about the perceived effects of the crack epidemic on future generations. However, scientific research has since debunked many of the exaggerated claims associated with the crack mother myth, highlighting the importance of separating fact from fiction in discussions about substance abuse and pregnancy. The following section summarizes some of the exaggerated myths surrounding crack cocaine including and its effects on babies, compared to alcohol use and cigarette smoke, the widespread panic and stigmatization fueled by media portrayal, the scientific inaccuracy of the myth, and the resulting criminalization and punitive policies targeting Black mothers who used crack cocaine during pregnancy:

- ❖ **Exaggerated Effects of Crack Cocaine**
    - The myth claimed that mothers who used crack cocaine during pregnancy would give birth to severely disabled and dysfunctional children, known as "crack babies," suffering from physical, developmental, and behavioral issues.
- ❖ **Alcohol and Cigarette Smoke**
    - While alcohol use during pregnancy leads to fetal alcohol spectrum disorders (FASDs) and smoking can cause complications such as respiratory problems and low birth weight, the media and public discourse did not sensationalize these issues to the extent they did with crack cocaine. Why?
    - Public health campaigns warning against alcohol and cigarette smoke during pregnancy have been less sensationalized and stigmatizing compared to Black mothers of crack babies. Why?
    - Punitive and criminal actions against mothers who engage in these behaviors have been less common compared to those aimed at mothers who used crack cocaine. Why?
- ❖ **Widespread Panic & Stigmatization**
    - The media exaggerated the effects of crack cocaine on babies, leading to widespread panic and stigmatization of mothers who used the drug.
    - News reports often depicted crack babies as irreparably damaged and portrayed their mothers as irresponsible and morally deficient.
- ❖ **Scientific Inaccuracy:**
    - The scientific inaccuracy of the crack baby myth lies in the exaggerated and often sensationalized claims about the effects of prenatal cocaine exposure on fetal

development. Pay attention here - while it is true that prenatal exposure to cocaine can have negative effects on fetal development, such as the potential for behavioral or cognitive issues and low birth weight, the myth portrayed these effects as severe, irreparable, and irreversible - suggesting that babies born to mothers who used crack cocaine during pregnancy would inevitably face lifelong challenges and disabilities. Lies.
- However, empirical data has shown that the actual extent of these effects is often more nuanced and can vary widely depending on factors such as maternal health, environmental and socioeconomic influences, and the dosage and timing of cocaine exposure. While there can be risks associated with prenatal cocaine exposure, the myth exaggerated these risks and contributed to stigmatization and misconceptions about affected individuals, namely Black women and their children (born and unborn).

❖ **Criminalization & Punitive Policies**
- The crack baby myth led to punitive policies targeting Black mothers who used crack cocaine during pregnancy.
- These policies included the criminalization of drug use during pregnancy and the removal of children from their mothers' custody based solely on drug use.

It's crucial to clarify that these comparisons are not intended to advocate for the criminalization of pregnant women who use substances other than crack cocaine. Nor do these comparisons seek to diminish the validity of any traumatic experiences, whether directly or indirectly linked to parental or cultural trauma resulting from crack addiction. Rather, the aim of these comparisons is to highlight the disproportionate targeting of Black women during the crack cocaine epidemic and genocide. Substance abuse among expectant mothers was observable across various socioeconomic statuses and racial and ethnic groups. However, Black communities had the greatest concentration of crack cocaine users. The crack baby myth was designed based on racists, exaggerated and often inaccurate beliefs about the effects of prenatal cocaine exposure. The myth led to harmful stigmatization and punitive actions against mothers and families, despite scientific and empirical evidence challenging many aspects of the myth. Instead of addressing the epidemic as a public health crisis and providing Black women with necessary treatment, they were unjustly criminalized, marginalized, maligned, and separated from their families and children.

The medical, scientific and empirical inadequacies which fueled the myths are astounding and extremely problematic. These myths were created by race-gendered, flawed, illogical hysteria. Primitive logic. Myths that continue to pervade our communities. If you're a second-generation trauma survivor like me, it's probable that these myths are also deeply connected to the shame you continue to carry to this day.

Are you with me?

Repeat after me.

"Black women cannot afford to be fools."

Say it again for the people in the back!

"Black women cannot afford to be fools."

To effectively challenge and "talk back" about our oppression, it's imperative to shift Black women from the margins of the crack cocaine epidemic and genocide and place them at the center of their lived experience to reclaim their truth. The truth is that any analysis and or dialogue that does not situate the crack cocaine epidemic (and victims lost) at the center of said genocidal, chemical, and biological warfare waged against the Black community does not serve us and is illogical, ignorant, and insufficient. The process of finding your voice, confronting your shadow, and deconstructing your beliefs are critical steps toward your healing journey. Now, it's your turn to embark on this journey of reclaiming your truth.

Applying The Sankofa Writing Method

Affirmation
My story is powerful, and I am ready to speak my truth

Putting Concepts into Action

The chapter discussed the importance of finding your voice, confronting shadows, and examining personal beliefs as crucial aspects of the healing journey. Drawing on bell hooks' concept of *"talking back"* as a form of resistance, it emphasizes the significance of articulating your story and challenging societal norms that silence marginalized groups, namely Black women. The chapter explores the process of confronting internalized beliefs and shadows, particularly regarding the portrayal of Black mothers and the crack baby myth. Now, it's your turn to apply what you've learned.

Writing Prompts

- ❖ Reflect on your shadows by identifying traits or aspects of yourself that you suppress or reject. How do these shadows manifest in your life, and what steps can you take to integrate them?
- ❖ Consider the concept of *"talking back"* as a form of resistance. How can expressing your truth challenge dominant power structures and reclaim agency?
- ❖ Consider a narrative or stereotype that has been perpetuated by societal norms or historical accounts. How has this narrative shaped your understanding of your family history?
- ❖ What gaps in knowledge are needed to help challenge your beliefs about your ancestors?
- ❖ Investigate the impact of societal stereotypes and controlling images on your identity and sense of self-worth. How

have these representations influenced your perceptions of yourself and your ancestors?
- ❖ Analyze the crack baby myth and its portrayal in the media. How has misinformation and sensationalization affected your personal beliefs?

Chapter 4
Excavate Trauma

Black women have had to develop a larger vision of our society than perhaps any other group. They have had to understand white men, white women, and black men. And they have had to understand themselves. When black women win victories, it is a boost for virtually every segment of society.
- Angela Davis

The next step in The Sankofa Writing Method is about excavating our trauma. In this chapter, we did deep—so that we can go back to the moments we have been fearful of discussing. This chapter delves into the process of excavation—a profound exploration into deeply buried truths of our personal and collective histories. Through excavation, we uncover the layers of intergenerational trauma, societal injustices, and historical legacies that have influenced our lives. It is through this *unraveling of the roots* which is required for us to apply what comes next for our healing journey.

Unraveling the Roots & Taking Inventory

It is important to note that the process of rewriting my mother's counter-future took time. This was not a quick fix, or an overnight process. It took me weeks to even begin drafting the first version of her counter-future. I was still in my feelings. I was still resentful about things my mother had done, and she transitioned in 2011. I was still holding onto *stuff*—physically and emotionally. My body was absorbing this pain. This healing process is a journey, and I mean that. I was trying to determine where to begin. In the end, I decided that to do this work, I needed to start from my pain. I needed to get to the root of *why* I did not talk about my mother. I needed to talk about my shame, and this did not feel good. I needed to start from the pain so that I could examine and question it. I gave myself a lot of grace and time. I was also doing this work while in conversation with another Black woman truth-teller, a thought partner, a healer and my therapist. Be mindful about your healing process, and take your time. You do not want to force any emotions that are not authentic. If you force it, it will not work. There are no shortcuts. This method is about taking inventory, seeking knowledge, and questioning our beliefs. You can do this. I know it to be true because I did it, and I will guide you along the way. So, let's get to work.

Critical Traumatic Incidents & Memory Work

This chapter is about exploring our journey of introspection and reflection, delving into *critical traumatic incidents,* and engaging in memory work to unravel the depths of our past experiences. I explore *critical traumatic incidents* as memories and experiences that trigger a trauma response as a result of experiencing trauma directly or indirectly. I'm talking about the moments when we were embarrassed, the moments we were violated, the moments we were left all alone, the moments we were in our heads, wishing this nightmare would stop, and for those moments we were in our head, asking "Why me?" So, let us explore it.

Memory work refers to a process of introspection and reflection aimed at exploring and understanding one's past experiences, emotions, and traumas. It involves delving into personal memories and recollections, often with the guidance of therapeutic techniques or practices to gain insight and growth. Examples of techniques include storytelling, journaling, and guided meditations—some of the strategies that we will use within this chapter. The goal of memory work is to uncover hidden or suppressed emotions, patterns, and beliefs, allowing individuals to process and make sense of their experiences to achieve greater self-awareness and healing.

The *critical traumatic incidents* that are selected in this step will be used later on in the healing journey. So, you want to be selective of the moments that you choose to engage with on a deeper level. Use your discernment. I chose moments that I knew I could describe really well. I chose moments that left scars because they were publicly humiliating for me, and I never talked about them. So, I wanted to use these moments as experiments to do this work. I also chose moments that I could write about without inflicting harm or violence toward my mother's body. Drawing from personal childhood memories, I selected a *critical traumatic incident* that left me feeling betrayed by my mother when she stole from me once. The writing sample below is unedited—this was a creative free-write and journal activity. The writing does not need to be perfect here. The goal is simply to write it out as it comes to you. A free flow of consciousness. I always tried to fill up an entire page, and if I didn't fill a page, I pushed myself to go deeper. Set a goal for yourself that pushes you to write as much as you can. If you write a sentence, that's great! You took a step. If you write a paragraph and need to stop and take a break, that's okay. Take your time. Take breaks. Do not worry about grammar and spelling. Do not spend too much time trying to figure out how to explain the incident. Describe it the way you would say it to yourself in plain language. For this activity, I did a combination of an audio recording and writing. Talking through my emotions and memories comes easier to me at times. Do what feels natural for you. Below is an example of my journal entry about a critical traumatic incident called '*Stolen Tapes*':

Stolen Tapes

One evening, when I was home alone with my Grandmother, there was a knock at the screen door. I was sitting in the living room watching TV, so I stood up and walked towards the front door. I let my mother in, after inspecting her appearance at the front door. Back then, I was accustomed to usually letting my grandmother decide if my mother was allowed in the home. As I got older, she began to trust my judgment and allowed me to determine if I wanted to let my mother in the house. I must have been around

11 or 12. Usually, a few different factors helped us discern if we should let her in. Usually, it was the overall temperament. My mother's mood and overall temperament were always indicators. It's interesting because I can't actually recall my grandmother ever sitting me down and telling me any of this. She never said, do not let her in if she looks like this, sounds like that. I just knew. It was a mutual code and level of understanding between grandmother and granddaughter that we will always protect this house and protect one another. She didn't appear to be off-balance. Her speech was clear. She looked "clean". Or clean enough to wonder where she had slept the night before.

Well, this day, I let my mother into the home. She stood in the living room and asked where my grandmother was. She was looking around. If memory serves, she was upstairs in her bedroom on the phone or out in the backyard hanging up clothes. I remember , my mother had this pacing about her. It was a pace that let me know that perhaps, I shouldn't have let her in. And then as quickly as I had told her that grandmother was in a distant enough room, she grabbed three VHS tapes off the television sitting in the living room. I remember those tapes well. Maybe a year prior, those tapes were a gift from an uncle. They were Looney Tune tapes, which (at the time) was one of our favorite cartoons. She was so fast. She took the tapes and as quickly as she had stepped inside of the house, she was already back out the door. I stood there confused and in shock. What would I do now? What should I do? Instinct told me to chase her down, and I did.

I chased my mother to the corner of our street, calling out her name and screaming, "Mommy, Mom, please bring back my tapes." She was already around the corner by the time I had gotten outside. I ran up the street yelling. Neighbors watched. I stopped at the corner and stood in the middle of the street. Further off in the distance, my mother turned back, holding my tapes, and she started laughing. She was laughing at me. Because she had won. I stood there, shaking my head. A puddle of mixed emotions of an adolescent girl. The range of emotions I felt were too much:

embarrassed, disappointed, betrayed, and upset that I failed at protecting my home. I didn't even notice my neighbor sitting on her front steps at the corner house. She was smoking a cigarette, and she had watched the whole thing transpire. She just shook her head and said, "I know your mother didn't just steal from you girl. What did she take? Are you okay?" I shook my head and said, "No" and slowly walked back to the house. Because now, I needed to tell my grandmother that my mother had just stolen from me.

Back then, everyone on the block knew your business. Everyone knew that my mother was a junkie. And I despised that my pain was always on what seemed to be a public display for my family and my neighbors. I felt like I needed to work really hard at managing my emotions when it came to my mother. I cried a lot when I was alone. I mostly just remember feeling deep shame and resentment toward her. I did my best to hide my shame. And I didn't want people feeling sorry for me. Usually, after an encounter, I'd get a flood of love and support from family. Uncles and aunts would tell me things like, "It's not your fault, your mother is just sick. You just keep going to school and be the best version of yourself that you can be. You are not your mother." I resented my mother. I hated that I came from her. But I would be ready the next time she came to this house. She would never steal a thing from me. Ever again.

I remember this day so vividly, and when I was writing about what I remembered, I wrote through it based on how I recalled feeling as a child. While I was narrating this memory, it is important to note that this was written after over two years of seeing my therapist. Emotionally—I was not triggered while discussing this memory at all. In fact, there were moments when I was actually laughing—because it was my mother, and I could laugh if I wanted to. She really stole my damn tapes and ran around the corner so fast. I was tired as hell chasing after my mamma!

You can laugh, Sis. Laughter is cathartic, and this is therapeutic because this is what we do—we laugh through our pain like Kevin Hart showed us with his own father, who suffered from his addiction. We need to laugh sometimes to get through it. We trauma bond over the crazy and insane things that our loved ones did. Our laughs give us temporary reprieve from the pain we really feel. Three things can be true all at once—we can love our ancestors dearly, we can be humiliated by their behaviors and actions, and we can laugh it off because we understand that they were not themselves. This journal entry caused me to remember what it felt like to try really hard to absorb all of my shame. I swallowed my tears publicly as a child, and I had forgotten what it was like navigating these moments. I never trusted my mother. I knew better, and I learned over the years to keep a watchful eye over her whenever she was in our home. I felt disappointed because I didn't protect my home. I felt sad about being betrayed by my mother, but I also felt like I had let my Grandmother down.

This memory work helped me to see that, in retrospect, I was a child—and I was not aware of the cognitive deficiencies that caused my mother to behave the way that she did. I was not aware of my mother's diagnosis of schizophrenia, bipolar disorder, and dementia and what these chronic disorders meant for her behavior. I was unaware that her behaviors were symptoms of chronic disorders that caused severe declines in cognitive functioning and impaired reasoning. So, my beliefs as a child were rooted in my (mis)understanding that my mother was choosing, lucidly, to steal from me. We'll talk more about the medical and physiological implications of crack cocaine on the brain in Chapter four. This is important so that we can locate our ancestors in their proper position by acknowledging their addictions as medical disorders as we contextualize and engage with these traumatic incidents.

Truth is truth. We will name truth for what it is. I will periodically provide reminders throughout this guide, almost as a recalibration. For me, I kept sliding in and out of this victimhood position. I was feeling the cognitive dissonance. It was almost as if I was resisting the urge to forgive my mother and to see her as the victim that she was. I was in a battle with myself over my beliefs and at every turn, I gleaned into logic, reasoning, and truth to snap me back to the center. As I said, this is a process. It was not easy for me. I believe that I am an intelligent individual capable of making sound decisions. However, my beliefs about my mother were so deeply rooted in mistruths, misperceptions, and ignorance that it took a lot of work to undo it. Had I known about the symptoms of my mother's medical cognitive disorders, my response to her stealing from me would have been extremely different.

Can you see it now? Do you understand why this excavation work is so important? Are you with me? I have shown you my truth. Now, it's your turn.

Let's continue.

Applying The Sankofa Writing Method

Affirmation
I release myself from past mistakes and embrace forgiveness as a path to healing and growth

Putting Concepts into Action

This chapter serves as a guide for excavating and navigating *critical traumatic incidents*, inviting readers to embark on a transformative journey of self-discovery and healing through the power of memory work. Now, it's your turn to apply the method by detailing *critical traumatic incidents* from your life. Remember, I focus on the crack epidemic to track my application of the method stemming from trauma tied to my mother's addiction. Apply this step toward any form of cultural trauma that you would like to work on and heal from. Begin by taking inventory of memories that were traumatic for you. You might also choose a memory that does not include a parent or loved one because they were not there. Maybe they couldn't be there because they transitioned too soon, or were slain at the hand of gun violence, or they overdosed at the height of their suffering, or were incarcerated. You might decide to choose a milestone. For example, my mother was not present for any milestone that I have *ever* had in my entire life. I'm talking about elementary school assemblies, choir performances, award ceremonies, graduations, sporting events, my wedding, and the birth of my children. My mother was not able to share any of these moments with me. If you have similar moments in your life, and the absence of your ancestor was traumatic for you, and you would like to explore that, then use it. Whatever it is. Name it for yourself and use this method as a tool that works for you.

Mindfulness Exercise

Find a comfortable seated position either in a chair with your feet flat on the ground or if you prefer, you can sit with your legs crossed on the floor or using a cushion. Close your eyes.
Begin by bringing your awareness to a critical traumatic incident that you have experienced. Allow the memory to come into your mind without judgment or resistance. Notice how this memory feels in your body. Pay attention to any sensations of tension, tightness, or discomfort that arise as you recall the incident.
Take slow, deep breaths, inhaling through your nose and exhaling through your mouth.
What color is the memory?
What energy does this memory have?
What emotion does this memory invoke?
What does the room feel like?
How do you feel at this moment?
If there are others in this memory, how are they feeling in this moment?
What do you think they are thinking about?
How do you feel about your ancestors in this memory?
How does everyone around you feel about your ancestor in this moment?
Think about the way you felt.
Tap into the energy of yourself in that memory.
Start from where you are.
With each exhale, imagine yourself releasing any stress or tension. As you continue to breathe deeply, focus on the areas of your body where

you feel stress or discomfort. Send your breath to these areas, allowing them to soften and relax with each breath.

Notice any thoughts or emotions that arise as you engage in this practice. Acknowledge them without judgment, and then gently guide your focus back to your breath. Consider the sensory details of this moment and visualize the physical environment.

Repeat this process of deep breathing and body awareness for several minutes, allowing yourself to fully experience the present moment without becoming overwhelmed by the memory.

When you feel ready, slowly open your eyes, and return your awareness to your surroundings.

Take a moment to notice how you feel after completing this meditation.

Writing Prompts

- ❖ List a *critical traumatic incident* that surfaced during your meditation about your ancestor. If several memories surfaced, just focus on writing about one for this activity.
- ❖ Consider the sensory details of this moment: What happened? What did it feel like? What did it smell like? Take note of any colors, textures, or sensations.
- ❖ Visualize the physical environment: Think about the details of the space you were in. Was the floor hard or soft? What color was the carpet? Who else was there? How did you and others in the room feel? What was said or exchanged during this moment?
- ❖ Write as much as you can. Try to write up to one page.
- ❖ Engage deeply with the memory: Allow yourself to fully immerse in the experience and be present in the moment.

Once done, you can repeat the process for other *critical traumatic incidents*, focusing on uncovering the nuances and details of each experience. Reflect on the insights gained from revisiting these memories and consider compiling a list of key takeaways or realizations.

Great job! This healing journey is not easy, and we just covered a difficult step. Do not be ashamed to cry thug tears if you need to. Baby, I spent most of 2023 crying tears of pain, sorrow, and joy. You are brave, and you are worthy. Remember, you are not alone.

Keep going. It only gets better.

Chapter 5

Destroy the Myths

Where does a Black woman go when she is me, trailed by myths that this country has invented about her? Where to go to, when all of you have been there already, and claimed the turf as your own and you watch the rest of us shipwrecked by circumstance and color, looking. Waiting. Needing.
~ Sonia Sanchez

I was always a lover of poetry and making words dance on a page. Nikki Giovanni and Sonia Sanchez are two of my favorite poets. My favorite poem by Nikki Giovanni is *Ego Tripping* and I had the privilege of meeting her once in 2004 while in undergrad at West Chester University (of PA). I was on the executive board of the Black Student Union, and we partnered with the Frederick Douglass Institute on campus to host her visit and public lecture. You know about the Frederick Douglass Institute at WCU right? It's the campus where Douglass gave his last public lecture on February 1, 1895, just 19 days before his death. Nikki Giovanni came and spoke life into us.

Made us think, and question what we know. Her words were darts. Poignant. She autographed copies of her new book of poetry titled *"Quilting the Black-Eyed Pea: Poems and Not Quite Poems."* I still have my book, and I read it frequently. I never got a chance to meet Dr. Sanchez. We lived in the same neighborhood for a time, and secretly, I wished that I would bump into her one day while shopping at the Greene Street produce market. It was the rhythm and rhetorical style of her writing that gathered you up. *"Queens of the Universe"* is insane! Black women, you should read it today if you haven't already—you will not be disappointed. When I would read Sonia Sanchez—it was like a call and response in my head. So, when Sonia Sanchez says "Answer me,"…you wait until it's your turn to respond. I read her work and poetry the same way that I read anything else. Searching for myself in the words, stretching it out, searching for solutions. So, while reading this quote, I narrowed in on the solution. When Sonia asks,

"Where does a Black woman go when she is me, trailed by myths that this country has invented about her"

The answer came to me. Destroy the myths.

The next step of The Sankofa Writing Method is all about destroying the myths and preserving our truth. This chapter centers on the necessary excavation work of recovering our ancestors' truths which allows us to create new language so that we may redefine them. Recovering their truth refers to the process of rediscovering and reclaiming authentic narratives and experiences that may have been obscured or suppressed by external influences, societal norms, or personal trauma. It involves unraveling layers of distortion and misinformation to unveil one's genuine identity, history and lived experiences. Recovering truth entails acknowledging and confronting the complexities of one's past, embracing vulnerability, and seeking to align one's understanding of self with an honest and genuine reflection of reality.

This work is complicated, because it is not new for us as Black women. We live our lives daily as walking, talking contradictions to these nonsensical myths. We've been defining ourselves for ourselves for generations—using our mother's tongue. Our definitions for ourselves fall on faint ears. But we move forward. Self-definition has been a touchstone that is central to Black feminist and womanist theory. A central tenet of Black feminist theory is the ability to challenge negative stereotypes, enabling Black women to define themselves. Self-definition allows us to recover and rearticulate our truths, while deconstructing the stigmas that position us as the *pejorative other*. My journey of "recovery" involved engaging in archival work to stay as close to my mother's truth as possible so that I could redefine and reclaim her legacy. Self-definition is the power to name one's own reality as a form of resistance and rejection of Eurocentric dominant portrayals and definitions of Black womanhood. By defining our experiences for ourselves, Black women thrive without being objectified or silenced. Acknowledgment and affirmation across Black women's networks play a crucial role in this process as a journey from internalized oppression to the "free mind" in the formation of the collective consciousness.

Understanding Margins & Centers

We can understand our location and the myths about us more clearly in the context of "margins and centers." Thank God for Black women intellectuals and truth-tellers for their brilliance. Master teacher bell hooks extensively explored the dynamics of privilege, power, and marginalization in her writings. In *"Feminist Theory: From Margin to Center,"* hooks highlights the importance of centering the perspectives and voices of marginalized groups, particularly women of color, within feminist activism and discourse. She developed a frame that called for a more inclusive and intersectional approach to feminism that took into account forms of oppression experienced by women at the "margins" of society. hooks wasn't alone—in fact, many Black women scholars, activists, and writers like Patricia Hill Collins, Angela Davis, and Audre Lorde have also contributed to discussions about "margins and centers" within academic and social discourses.

In her seminal work, *"Mapping the Margins: Intersectionality, Identity Politics, and Violence Against Women of Color,"* scholar, activist, and civil rights advocate Dr. Kimberlé Crenshaw in her brilliance articulates the concept of intersectionality—where she maps the interconnected nature of oppression(s) and isms, such as sexism, classism, racism, to amplify the urgency in centering the experiences of marginalized groups who exist at the intersections.

Our work to center ourselves is about defining ourselves and adopting inclusive approaches to social justice advocacy. Imagery is a powerful tool for me, so whenever I hear "margin and center" —I can see it in my mind. For those like me who can benefit from visual aids, below is a figure that captures our positionality and our location on the margins:

Margin to Center:

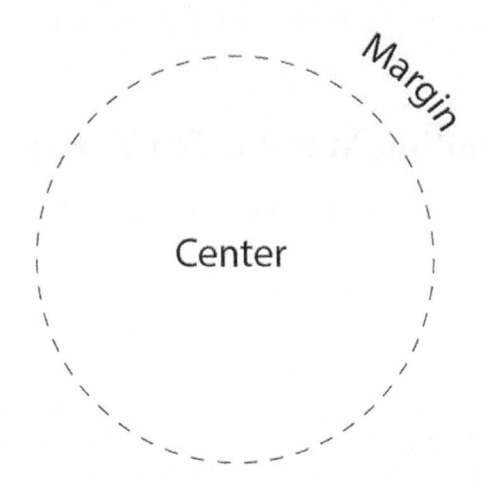

(Figure: a dashed circle labeled "Margin" along its perimeter, with "Center" written inside.)

So, what does this mean? For me, it meant that I had to completely do away with "what I thought" I knew about my mother because I realized that my beliefs were not my own. My beliefs about my mother were rooted in myths and mistruths. I perpetuated the myths because I did not know any better and I subscribed to the dominant narratives invented about her. I needed to name the beliefs that I felt about myself as a girlchild that I never reconciled as a result of being born to her. I needed to name it. Explicate it. I needed to see it. I needed to map it. So that's what I did. I journaled about these myths. Drawing circles and scribbling words. It was happening. I was trying to develop a framework. I drew two circles, one for myself and one for my mother. Both circles were labeled 'Myth.' The following figure captures an example of what this circle looks like:

○ Myth

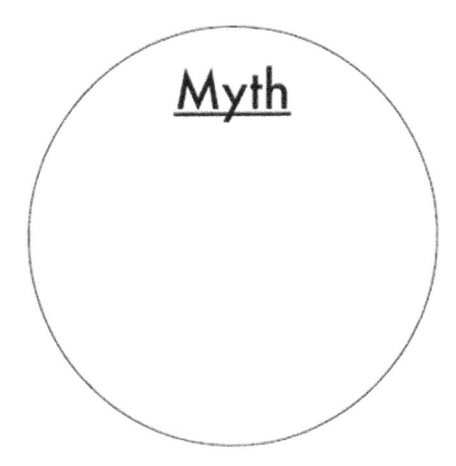

In the center of the first circle, I wrote down my beliefs about myself and the crack baby myth, which were influenced by mainstream and societal views:

- ❖ Not being good enough
- ❖ Not being worthy
- ❖ Not being smart
- ❖ Not being valued
- ❖ Not being wanted

As a girlchild, I feared that I wouldn't be seen as good enough or worthy enough because of the stigmas associated with the 'crack baby' myth. I questioned if I was smart enough, and I was afraid of being abandoned and disposed of, so I gave myself little error so that I did not disappoint the elders. Pay attention here. There was never, ever, ever any real threat or a moment when anyone in my family ever said to me that I was not good enough, that I was not worthy, that I was not smart, and that I was not wanted. My fears were rooted in an outcome that would never occur because my fears were not real. I made them real with my beliefs, so I pleased others to keep them happy because I could see how much my mother's addiction hurt them. So, I made good choices, giving myself very little room for error. I worked hard at not becoming a burden for anyone. At every turn, I chose the better decision so that I could move forward. A girl on the run. It was an irrational belief. I subscribed to it. I made life decisions that were informed by this belief that was not real. It was a myth. An irrational and illogical belief.

In the second circle, I detailed myths about my mother that were also rooted in dominant worldviews about Black crack mothers:

- ❖ Neglectful "bad" parent who was lucidly choosing to neglect her children
- ❖ Promiscuous and hypersexual
- ❖ Lazy, and not seeking the help she needed
- ❖ She was to be blamed for her behavior

As a girlchild, I believed my mother neglected us and that she was choosing to leave us and never return. I thought she was a bad parent because she never really spoke to me and asked me questions or how I was doing. I thought she was choosing to live a life apart from us. I believed that she was responsible to some degree, even through her sickness, and that she deserved to be blamed. None of these things are true because my mother never gave consent for these things. These beliefs were illogical. They were myths. They held some truth for my lived experience, but I was not humanizing my mother's lived experience, which was that she was cognitively impaired and in dire need of treatment and support. So, I held these myths in my hand, and I examined them as I had always done. One by one. I deconstructed each belief that was rooted in the dominant worldview and narrative about my mother and myself. I did this in conversation with my therapist. Because I knew better - my ego had no place here. There was work to be done. So, I *Shapeshifted* and became a container for my mother and for myself.

Therapy Sessions

So, I don't know what you all talk about with your therapists! But baby—me and mine—we go DEEP! Our sessions were everything I needed. I looked forward to them. My therapist taught me to name my beliefs and narrow down my emotional triggers to them, which resulted in behaviors. She told me about the cognitive triangle, which is a conceptual model used in cognitive behavioral therapy because it was important for me to understand that thoughts, beliefs, and behaviors influence one another. Theory was my love language, so I did what I had always done. I studied that cognitive triangle down to the tee. My therapist taught me that my thought patterns created cognitive scripts, and she explained that these scripts were like loops—just a cycle going round and round. She explained that by altering my thoughts about my mother, these thought patterns would lead to corresponding changes in my emotions and behaviors. She helped me to see that my beliefs about my mother and my thoughts about my mother were triggered by situations that set the cognitive triangle in motion. For those like me who need to see what this looks like, here is a chart provided by Therapist Aid LLC that really helped me to understand:

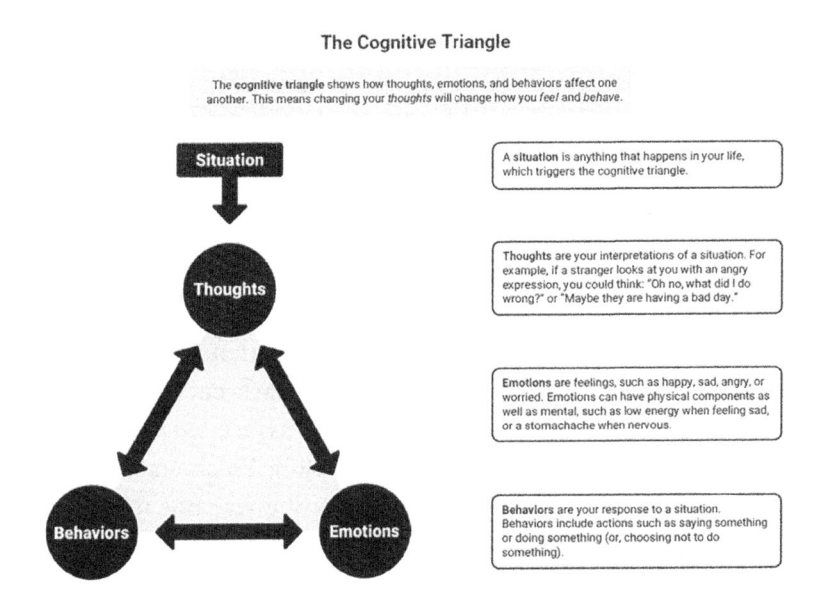

The Cognitive Triangle

The **cognitive triangle** shows how thoughts, emotions, and behaviors affect one another. This means changing your *thoughts* will change how you *feel* and *behave*.

A **situation** is anything that happens in your life, which triggers the cognitive triangle.

Thoughts are your interpretations of a situation. For example, if a stranger looks at you with an angry expression, you could think: "Oh no, what did I do wrong?" or "Maybe they are having a bad day."

Emotions are feelings, such as happy, sad, angry, or worried. Emotions can have physical components as well as mental, such as low energy when feeling sad, or a stomachache when nervous.

Behaviors are your response to a situation. Behaviors include actions such as saying something or doing something (or, choosing not to do something).

So, we deconstructed every belief. We were destroying the myths. She was helping me to see that my beliefs were rooted in subconscious, irrational, and maladaptive thoughts. We were thought partners on this journey. My therapist had the answers, and it was truth and logic that made me see. During my sessions, I shared with her that my mother's addiction started right after it was said that my mother was "Slipped a mickey" in one of her drinks one day. It was a story that I heard growing up— but I never really processed what that really meant for my mother and her life. My therapist and I excavated. Dug deep. We explored the phrase "Slipped a mickey" and talked about its reference to the act of someone secretly adding a drug, usually a sedative or incapacitating substance, to someone else's drink without their knowledge or consent. Being slipped a mickey is a colloquial phrase—similar to "date rape" drugs, leaving victims vulnerable to sexual assault. Slipping someone a mickey was done with the intention of rendering the person unconscious or incapacitated to take advantage of them. This was not new information, but I was engaging with this information very differently now.

Wait.

I sat with that. I thought about it. I put it in the palm of my hand and I examined it. So, my mother was robbed of her ability to give consent, and that drink would trigger a downward spiral?

Black women are truth-tellers. My therapist helped me to see something that was there all along. I always heard the story of my mother getting slipped a mickey—but as a child, I did not make the connection about my mother never having the ability to consent. A truth re-realized. A memory. A fact that I had forgotten. Not only was my mother a victim of the crack cocaine epidemic and genocide and the harmful pathologies associated with what it meant to be a Black woman, who was also a Black crack mother, but my mother never ever gave consent. She was not involved in the decision-making process to engage in this death threat awaiting in her cup. She never agreed. Never gave her permission. She was a victim of being robbed of her joy and her innocence. She didn't have a choice. She never had a fucking chance. I was enraged for her—but I had never thought of her circumstances in this way.

Ever.

Black women are truth-tellers. My therapist helped me to see something that was there all along. I would describe my mother as "child-like" in our sessions, and my therapist would say:

"Because she was."

I did not understand, so she proceeded to make me see it. She started breaking down the technology and the science of neurology, and she talked about how the brain works, and then she began telling me about the prefrontal cortex, which is the front part of the brain's cerebral cortex, located just behind the forehead. She talked about this part of the brain being the last to mature and described it as the "personality center" —playing a crucial role in cognitive functions, such as problem-solving, planning, impulse control, decision-making, and social behavior. We talked about how sensitive this part of the brain was developmentally between adolescent years through the age of 25. We talked about how important it was for parents to understand how sensitive this part of the brain was for their teenagers and their ability to develop cognitively.

She explained that when users became addicted to crack cocaine at young ages, their cognitive maturation was disrupted. Leaving them stuck. If they were addicts as teenagers, their executive brain functioning would be that of a teenager. Crack cocaine use had severe effects on the prefrontal cortex, which is responsible for cognitive functions and decision-making processes. Addicts were cognitively functioning based on the age they were when they became addicted and based on the maturation of the prefrontal cortex.

Exhale.

So, my entire life, when I felt like my mother was being annoying, disrespectful, and dishonoring our family, neglecting her children, and mutilating her body, and when I was describing her as "child-like" —it was because *she was?*

Cognitively, her ability to make decisions, her ability to access her memory, her ability to problem-solve, and her ability to control her impulses were limited. Medically, she was stuck in place. The brain damage had a severe impact over time, depending on how severe the abuse of the substance was. So, when my mother was slipped a mickey without her consent, she spent the rest of her life searching for that first hit. And cognitively, she was unable to stop.

We talked about the effects of chronic drug use and how they can alter the brain's structure and function—this is a process called neuroplasticity. Major changes in the synaptic connections in the brain can lead to long-lasting alterations in behavior and cognition, making it difficult for individuals to quit using drugs *even when they want to.*

Even when they want to.

Even when they want to.

It was so messed up that I had to write it twice. Brain damage caused by crack cocaine impaired decision making and the brain's executive functions, including impulse control and self-regulation.

Are you with me?

These impairments caused by the brain damage as a result of being an abuser of crack cocaine, after being slipped a mickey in which you gave no consent, can lead to risky behaviors, poor judgment, and difficulty resisting drug cravings. Emphasis added on "risky behaviors" —because I know for goddamn sure, there was no way my mother would have chosen geekin' and freakin' in somebody's crack house over raising her children and spending time with her family.

Are you with me?

Exhale.

Now, I could see it. I could see my mother's victimhood. I could see her humanity, and I could see that she never had a chance. Our people never had a chance. Black people. With families. With children. With jobs. Black women were serving as blood mothers, kin-mothers, and othermothers to their families and communities. These Black women, and Black people were minding their business. These Black people made grave decisions and hung out at the party for too long. They were seduced by an escape from the poverty they were already experiencing. They were seduced by the lack of jobs available. They were seduced by the disruption of public service programs. They were seduced because of reduced government spending and welfare benefits, leaving families to struggle to make ends meet, exacerbating poverty in marginalized communities. They did not know.

Exhale.

Our people did not know that crack cocaine usage can dysregulate the brain's stress response system, which leads to increased sensitivity to stress and negative emotions. They didn't know that the dysregulation of the brain's stress response system results in depression, anxiety, and other mental health disorders. All of which may further perpetuate drug use. They did not know that their addiction caused them to have *mental health* episodes.

Mental health. Did we say those words together in the late 80s and early 90s? Did we pair those two words together in our daily chit-chat on the subway, heading to school? Heading to work as we thought about our mothers? We call these mental health episodes now.

That language was not used for my mother. Mental health my ass. Societal narratives were not talking about my mother's emotional, psychological, and social well-being. Society did not examine my mother's mental health state and how it was influenced by environmental and social factors. Society did not see my mother as someone who deserved recourse and treatment. Society saw my mother as someone who should be blamed for her addiction. When she never gave consent.

Slipping Away

My mother had a lot of mental health episodes
Publicly
Shredding family pride
Breaking our hearts
And there was nothing we could do
But stand by
And watch in horror
As our mothers were being murdered
We stood and watched in horror
As our mothers died, slowly
As they slipped away
Falling
Through the cracks

Exhale.

Our people were so unaware of what this chemical would do to them, what it would do to their brains. So unequivocally unaware of the chemical and biological storm coming their way. They were not cautioned. So oblivious to the structural genocide brewing. They were oblivious. Young and free. Looking forward to watching the game on the weekend. Trying to figure out what number they would play for the lottery. Trying to go to work, to put food on the table. Trying to party on the weekends, because they worked all week. They didn't know this chemical would leave them frozen.

Then my therapist said:

"*We didn't know. No one knew.*"

Who didn't know? I asked her to explain it to me, and she did. Medically, there was no way to understand the severe effects that crack cocaine would have on the brain because the technology did not exist yet. The technology did not exist in the late 80s and early 90s. It wouldn't be until years later.

Years later. Years later.

Years later, when magnetic resonance imaging, we call it the MRI machine, would become widely accessible across medical institutions across the country. It would be years before any substantial and longitudinal data and medical research would paint a more accurate picture.

MRIs are diagnostic tools that provide us with valuable information about the anatomy and function of the body. Medical research was expanding because of the advancement of technology. How wonderful it was. Magnetic resonance could differentiate cancer cells from non-cancerous cells—the device was used to visualize various structures and tissues within the body with high detail and clarity. Magnetic resonance allowed doctors to diagnose and monitor conditions affecting the brain, including tumors, strokes, multiple sclerosis, Alzheimer's disease, and other neurodegenerative disorders.

My mother had a few of those neurodegenerative disorders. She suffered from dementia caused by the degeneration of the frontal and temporal lobes of the brain, which impacted her behavior, personality, language, and emotional processing. Symptoms include language difficulty and impaired cognition. My mother also suffered from schizophrenia, which usually involves delusions and hallucinations—meaning she was seeing and hearing things that did not exist. My mother talked to herself, and would impulsively cry, scream out, and laugh nervously. I hated her laugh as a child. I always thought she was laughing *at* us. I was uninformed. I did not realize her truth. Her physical behavior was unusual because she had no control over her thinking and speech patterns. She was paranoid because she could not control her thoughts. Wandering the streets. Hearing voices. Late at night. Looking for that next hit. Selling her soul for that next hit. My mother also contracted

HIV, which is the human immunodeficiency virus that attacks the body's immune system. There is no effective cure. Once she had it, she would have it for life.

My mother's body was mutilated. For decades her spirit was stolen. Of all the places my mother could have died, she transitioned in what I perceived to be the safest place on Earth for her. She died in a hospital, and my God—that was a gift. I was grateful that she was not anywhere else. I had nightmares about the places where she could have been found dead. I spent decades of my life dreading that phone call. She was safe and unharmed. She died of congestive heart failure at the age of 57 years old. Too young to become an ancestor. During the 24 hours leading up to my mother's death, she was surrounded with her loved ones—her mother, her children, her sisters, and her brother. A gift. Divine timing. We decided to visit her in a nursing home just a few weeks before her 58th birthday. For the first time ever, I celebrated my mother's birthday. We brought her balloons. Cake. We listened to music. We laughed. Surrounded her and covered her with kisses. We were loud *all up and through* that nursing home. It was the most beautiful day. Hours passed, and we were there with her when her discomfort arose—leading to our request for an ambulance to take her to the nearest hospital immediately. We were with her—by her side throughout the evening and night. Later, as my brother and I were heading home, we received a call from the hospital informing us that my mother went into cardiac arrest shortly after we all had left.

Exhale.

I was driving on the highway when we received the call. The rest is a blur. I needed to pull over so that I could scream. I pulled over alongside the highway, and we cried in the darkness. Unable to drive, my brother took over as we returned back to the hospital. When we arrived, we identified my mother's body, and one of the doctors asked if we would approve the donation of her body to HIV and AIDS research.

"No."

Her body was ours. Our mother was ours.

Exhale.

My therapist gave me the tools to see my mother's victimhood. Her humanity. I took notes in our sessions and became a student. I studied the medical terms that were foreign to me because I needed to know them. I needed to understand how drug use impacted the brain so that I could map it to the diagnostic capabilities made available through the advancement of medical technology offered through magnetic resonance imaging. I needed to understand the chemical makeup of the substance and how it was used. I needed to know this so that I could understand that when cocaine was smoked, it was rapidly absorbed into the pulmonary circulatory system, which is a medical term describing the network of blood vessels that carries blood between the heart and the lungs. I needed to know that when cocaine was smoked, it transmitted to the brain in less than ten seconds, giving a high that lasted about five minutes.

Ten seconds. Five minutes.

So little time. I needed to understand why my mother did the things that she did. I needed to understand her behaviors and how she went crazy. I needed to understand *why* she became stuck after never giving consent. I needed to understand what it meant when I would hear people say that crack users felt an extreme high or a "crash." What the fuck was a crash? What did that mean chemically, and what was happening in the brain? I never thought to ask these types of questions before. I needed to know so that I could map it to my beliefs. I needed to understand the physiology of crack cocaine use so that I could understand the difference between the regular snorting of cocaine, which may cause addiction over a few years, compared to smoking cocaine which caused addiction within a few months. I needed to understand that using crack cocaine increases behavior leading to its use and abuse—causing mood elevation briefly, followed by a deep psychological depression or "crash," leaving users wanting more. I needed to understand exactly how cocaine influences dopamine levels in the brain, which then changes brain activity, resulting in compulsive intense cravings. Cravings that would render my mother spiritless and completely out of control. Cravings that became more important than anything else in her life. I scoured data reported through the National Institute on Drug Abuse, the National Institute of Mental Health, and the National Household Survey on Drug Abuse so that I could understand the data and the trends. So that I could understand my mother's truth.

My mother needed help, and I wished those goddamn MRI machines had come just a decade sooner.

Distress Call

I wish those goddamn MRI machines came just a decade sooner
I wish the MRI machines came just a decade sooner
I wish that we had the longitudinal data
Because then, maybe the data could have saved our ancestors
Because then, maybe the data would have screamed out their truth
Which was that they needed help
We needed help
This is a distress call
We were given the tools to annihilate our communities
Then the media painted us as monsters
Our families needed help

Exhale

I wish that we had the data, so that the data could tell our truth
So that science could have helped to tell the truth from the margins
The truth from the margins
I wish the data could have sent a distress call
To save my mother
To save our mothers

I wish that we weren't chemically and biologically attacked
I wish that we had the data, to tell our truth
Which was that these women, were our mothers
These men were our fathers
These humans, these humans, these people had children
These people had babies
And you didn't have the data
You didn't have the longitudinal data
You did not have the data
You created public health policies that were not informed by longitudinal data
How?
You created public health policies with no understanding of the patterns, and trends, that would have been needed to have been measured, and tested, and measured, and tested again
You didn't have the longitudinal data
To even understand the disease outcomes
But you called our mothers monsters
Then you said, the dead babies may be the lucky ones
You actually said "the dead babies may be the lucky ones"
You didn't have the data

Exhale

This is a distress call
Our people were in distress
I wish the data could have sent a distress call
I wish that we had the longitudinal data to track disease progression
I wish that we had the longitudinal data to track trends with repeated measurements
I wish that we had the longitudinal data to assess treatment efficacy
I wish that we had the longitudinal data to tell the story of what was happening in my mother's brain. I wish the data could have saved our lives.
You called us monsters. Then you blamed us.
But you did not have the longitudinal data.
I really wish those MRI machines came just a decade sooner.
Because maybe, just maybe, they could have saved my mother's life.

I *disintegrated* the myths.

In Search of My Mother's Truth

Black women are truth-tellers, and my therapist made me see it. I embraced my mother's victimhood and held it tight. I was ready to fight. Because I knew bone deep that this was not what my mother would have chosen for herself, today, I can say that I know it to be true. Because my elders told me to speak up and to go out and learn all that I could. So, I did. And I knew that it was time for me to go and find my mother's truth. So, I searched for my mother's truth through the people who knew her best. I relied on family and loved ones to help fill in the gaps for me. I needed these stories. This data. I needed the details. I needed a witness, and this was urgent. I needed to ask new questions. So, I did. I needed to rekindle with her best friends when they were girlchildren so that I could see my mother's innocence. So, I did. I absorbed information differently now. And it changed my life. At my mother's funeral in 2011, I always remembered the woman who was adorned in her beautiful Muslim garb as she stood at the microphone on the pool pit of the church speaking about my mother. She was so incredibly heartbroken, and her voice was shaking as she tried to hold in her tears. She loved my mother. She was my mother's best friend since they were little girls. They grew up right next door to one another. She saw my mother's humanity, and I thanked her that day for her touching words and memories that she gave in honor of my mother. I had been wanting to reconnect with my mother's best friend for over ten years, but I never did. I was too busy *rippin' and running*. Time is fleeting. Time does not wait forever. So, I snatched the moment, and I finally reached out to her. Speaking with my mother's best friend changed me. Black women are truth-tellers, and I discovered a version of my mother I never knew.

Drumming & Snowstorms

*While speaking with my mother's best childhood friend
We talked about my mother's love for music at an early age
She shared that one of her favorite memories was during a snowstorm
when the streets were completely blocked with snow
It was 1966, 1967, or maybe it was 1968
It didn't matter, what mattered is that there was so much snow
that it came all the way up to the living room windows
So, everyone came outside to play and have snowball fights
She said that my mother brought her drum-set outside
Sat it right on top of the snow, and started playing music for the entire block
She recalled the Christmas lights that lit up the streets
And everyone was dancing to my mother playing the drums
In the snow, during the snowstorm
She described it as a joyous time
She said my mother's favorite artist was Santana
While everyone else was listening to Marvin Gaye, and Earth Wind and Fire
My mother insisted on listening to Santana
She loved animals, and had a little gray poodle named, Gigi
She felt like my mother never had a chance to rebound
after her addiction
She said "Your mother's heart was made of pure gold"
She described my mother as soft spoken, extremely friendly, and naïve
– with a big heart.
She was always smiling and laughing
Sweet and genuine. A generous soul.
She would give you her last dollar. She would give away
anything she had.
She said "Your mother had a soft heart…And people with soft hearts
get taken advantage of."
She attributed my mother's downfall to trusting others too easily.
My mother was pretty, with long black shiny hair
She said, "She was Gorgeous! But she didn't choose this on her own"
She said that "whatever demons she had, I'm telling you, not even a
tablespoonful of it was on her own. It was not on her own."*

Black women are truth-tellers. I am grateful to still have family who can fill in the voids for me. Speaking with loved ones and listening to them share stories that I was now *willing* to receive was cathartic. I listen differently now. On my quest to destroy the myths, I was in search of my mother's truth, and I relied on loved ones to provide it. Now, it is your turn.

Let's continue.

Applying The Sankofa Writing Method

Affirmation
I affirm my commitment to preserving and celebrating the truth of my ancestors' experiences

Putting Concepts into Action
In this chapter, we explored the powerful act of dispelling myths surrounding ourselves and our ancestors as a form of resistance and reclaiming their true identities. I shared my journey of identifying the myths I had internalized and those propagated by society about myself and my mother. Recognizing that these beliefs were based on falsehoods, I delved into the truth, viewing her addiction scientifically as a medical condition and chronic illness. By piecing together memories and stories from those close to her, I began to see a more holistic picture of who she truly was. In this chapter, we covered the importance of honoring our ancestors' humanity and preserving their legacies. Through this process, we rise above the constraints of addiction, allowing the genuine essence of our loved ones to shine. Your task is to explore the authentic truth of your ancestors, uncovering insights and understanding from a fresh perspective. Each detail revealed brings us closer to reclaiming and honoring their true essence. Now, it's your turn to apply these lessons and embark on your own journey of discovery.

Mapping Your Myths

It is important that we name our beliefs so that we may examine them. Using the following chart, begin to make a list of the myths that you subscribe to for yourself and your ancestor within the center of the circle. In the outer margin circle, begin to write what was actually true based on what you learned and what you remembered about your ancestor.

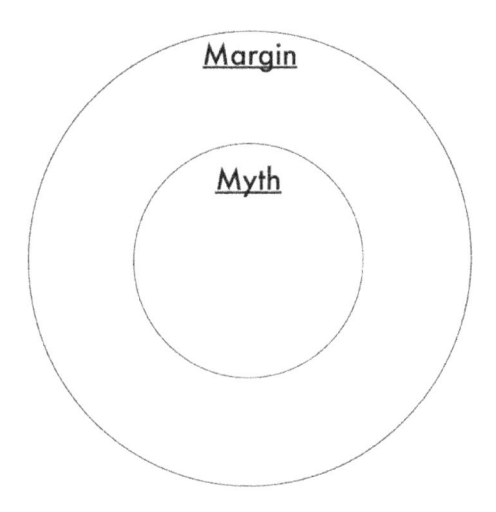

Circle diagram with outer ring labeled "Margin" and inner circle labeled "Myth"

Writing Prompts

❖ Write a list of at least three individuals who could help fill the void and provide you with truth about your ancestors before their struggle with addiction. Consider speaking with family members, friends, or coworkers of your loved one who may hold valuable insights into your ancestor's life. If you want to speak with more than three people, go for it. The goal is to get as close to the truth as possible.

❖ Next, you should craft a series of questions aimed at uncovering different aspects of your ancestor's identity and experiences before their addiction. Delve deep into their childhood, favorite songs, cherished memories, and personality traits. Spend some time thinking about exactly what it is you want to know. For example, in the 70s, my mother impulsively moved to Los Angeles, California with her boyfriend who was a musician and lived there for a short while. Wild and free. I also moved to California pretty abruptly with my family because we wanted a new life. This was always ironic and interesting to me, so I asked others about my mother's move to California. Be intentional in your questions. You'll be amazed by the information you'll uncover.

❖ Schedule dedicated time to meet with the individuals on your list. Approach these conversations with an open heart and a genuine curiosity for learning about your ancestor's life. Take note of the insights shared and the stories recounted, recognizing each detail uncovered as a valuable step towards reclaiming and honoring your ancestor's truth. If you feel comfortable, ask if you can record the conversation.

❖ Reflect on the process of exploring your ancestor's life, pre-addiction. Consider how these insights have deepened your understanding of their identity and enriched your connection to your family's history. How do these newfound revelations shape your perception of your ancestor and their journey? How do these newfound revelations shape you and your journey?

Chapter 6
Amplify The Margin

One of the serious flaws in Western logic, thought and scholarship is the failure or inability to see things as a "whole." Rather, the tendency is to perceive fragmented "abstractions" that are never united as one. This pattern of thought is sharply contrasted to the Eastern mode of thinking and perception that <u>begins</u> with the perception and analysis of the whole, so as to place in accurate perspective any parts or fragments which may be isolated from the whole.
~ Dr. Frances Cress Welsing

Sometimes, I just wish that I could sit, have coffee, and chit-chat with my ancestors. Dr. Welsing was out of control! I digress. The next step in the Sankofa Writing Method is to capture our ancestors as "whole" by amplifying the margin, by amplifying the truth. bell hooks' notion of "margin to center" is resistance work that forces us to shift the voices and experiences of the oppressed to the forefront. Centering marginal voices involves elevating the experiences of individuals who have historically been relegated to the margins of society due to their gender, sexuality, race, class, or physical ability. This work is about challenging systemic oppression, dominant narratives, and power structures to promote social justice and inclusivity. There is beauty and humanness within the margins. By centering our marginal experiences, we center our truths. The business of redressing our ancestors requires us to acknowledge their victimhood and honor their humanity.

Portrayals of Black Women Addicts in Popular Culture

Take a moment and think about dominant portrayals of Black women suffering from addiction in the media and across popular culture. How are they often depicted? I won't name the movies that come to mind. You know them. I spent some time thinking about this, and most of the depictions (whether it's through music, the media, or cinema) show Black women as desperate, strung out, poor, and lacking agency and dimension—which perpetuates the reinforcement of negative stereotypes about addiction. These depictions often ignore the complex factors contributing to substance abuse, such as historical trauma, socioeconomic disparities, and systemic oppression, thereby neglecting the humanity and individual experiences of Black women who struggle with addiction. In the previous chapter, we destroyed the dominant myths and broke down our beliefs about them. In this chapter, we amplify the marginal lived experiences of the oppressed so that we can center them and capture a more holistic picture of their experience.

As we acknowledge our trauma, articulate our experiences, and contextualize the systemic factors that perpetuated our ancestors' subjugation, we allow ourselves to see new truths. This process prompts us to ask new questions. Once I recognized my mother's humanity, I felt a range of emotions, including deep empathy, guilt, and anger. I felt terrible about the resentment that I held for her in my mind, body, and spirit all these years. This realization triggered memories long forgotten, unveiling layers of complexity in our shared history. Yet, as I delved deeper into her story, I came to understand that I had always seen her humanity; it was merely obscured by the weight of societal narratives and stigmas surrounding addiction. One memory that I recalled was when I chose to see my mother through the perspective of one of my elders: through the lens of my grandmother's sister-in-laws. One of the matriarchs and operators of my family's homeplace. My great aunt Julia:

Lessons From my Great Aunt Julia

I learned a lot from the elders in my girlhood
My great Aunt Julia would sit in her rocking chair
Watching the afternoon news, 6 ABC
One leg was amputated, and her wig sat on the table right beside her
Too much sugar
She rocked in that chair using her good leg
She had a little stutter, and she made the best pound cake, moist and thick
Her secret was the cream cheese
She had wall to wall green carpeting and floral wallpaper
In the living room, her couch was covered in plastic
Sometimes, we'd get stuck, and break out in sweats during afternoon naps in the summertime
She would sit in her rocking chair and tell me how precious I was
She called me her "doll baby" and I always felt stronger when I was around her
Because she was always fussin'
Always correcting our posture and our speech
It didn't matter if she were talking to us kids, or my aunts and uncles
She taught us all to speak up, and to sit up straight
Matriarchs making corrections
It truly was a marvel to witness this intergenerational exchange as a girlchild

"Stop leaning forward or you'll get a hunchback"
"Chew with your mouth closed"
"Cross your legs"
"Speak up!"
"If you talk real low, people won't be able to hear you"
"Fix your pants"
"Don't say ain't"
"Do this, don't do that"
"Speak Up!"

She gave me money from her bra and told me to never leave it all in one place
She had money stashed all over her house
Fussin' and adjusting everyone
Imparting information
Making us stronger
No matter what it was, she had the remedy
An herbalist
Unbothered
Unbreakable
Fearless
Acute
Precise
Correcting perfunctory behavior
Uninterested in personal boundaries
Molding us – like she was *shaping a newborn baby's head*
When we were sick as kids, we were sent to Aunt Julia's house to get better
Natural healer. She had the remedies.
She cut up onions, and put them everywhere
At night, she sat onions on the nightstand and put them in my socks to break my fevers
She kept her remedies stored away up in her medicine cabinet
Told me to go up in that cabinet and grab the cod liver and castor oil when I had stomach pain
Or a seasonal cold
Or a mosquito bite
Made me take a few sips of garlic water before bed
Made me brush my teeth with baking soda and peroxide
She knew what was going on in every room in her house at any given moment
She could see everything
She was a *Shapeshifter*
She knew exactly where everything was in her house
She taught me about the power of our memory
She told me to go out and learn all that I could, so that one day, I could be the smartest in the room

Elders teaching the children to use their brains
Testing and evaluating how well we were using them
In one breath, she'd say,

'Ayana, pay attention
Go upstairs, in the middle room,
look in the 2nd drawer in the closet closest to the window,
look up under them navy blue pants folded up in the
back right corner,
look in the left pocket, and pass me that envelope'

"Yes Mam"

Then I'd go skipping up the stairwell because walking took too long
Tryna' use my memory like she taught me to
Repeating the steps in my mind as I journeyed forth on this quest
I followed her guidance to a tee
I went into the middle room, and spotted the dresser by the window
The window was open – letting in a cool breeze
I spied a fly, sitting on the window seal
Watching me
I smiled at it, and swatted it away
It flew around the room, keeping watch as I checked each drawer looking for the navy-blue pants
The fly landed on the dresser, smiling back at me
Found it!
I found the drawer that had the navy-blue pants, and there was the envelope in the exact spot where my Great Aunt Julia said it would be
I was amazed
In awe of her superpower
She could see everything
At all times
I went flying down the stairwell at record speed because kids must run everywhere

"Got it"

She'd look at me and smile. She said, *"I know"*
Then she'd asked me if I had seen my mother in the neighborhood

"Yes mam"

She'd shake her head, and say, *"It's terrible what's happening to these young people. That's still your mother, she's just sick."*

She would lean forward in her chair, putting weight on her good leg
Then she asked if my mom had been over to the house for a hot meal lately

"Yes mam"

She sat back in her chair, using her good leg to start rocking again
Satisfied at my answer
She studied me, and nodded her head in approval

"Mmhmm that's right. Good. Good."

My Great Aunt Julia was making sure we were continuing the tradition
Then she opened up that envelope
Passed me two crisp $20 bills
Told me to roll it up real small, and put it in my overnight bag

"Give this to your Grandmother when you get home, and don't tell anyone else about it"

"Yes Mam"

Elders.
Sisters.
Shapeshifters.
Operators of our homeplace.
Bloodmothers. Othermothers.

Keeping a watchful eye over the children.

I spent weekends with my great aunt Julia. Her home was an *otherhome*. Through my aunt Julia's lens, my mother was a victim. The elders knew it. They perceived what was happening to my mother and "these young people" as something horrible and targeted. So, on weekends, the elders took turns keeping a watchful eye over my big brother and me. We became explorers of every neighborhood around the city. *Grandmas Kids.* Learning different ways of living. My relatives were always checking in and finding a way to talk about my mother to me. I was given positive affirmations from my aunts and uncles. I never spoke negatively about my mother. I knew better. No matter how difficult things were, speaking down about my mother was not something that was tolerated in my family. Not if I wanted to keep *all of my teeth that is*! I recalled these memories with relatives and one memory led to another as I continued to reframe experiences with my mother. I forced myself to think about moments when my mother experienced love, grace, and tenderness. Then I remembered, these moments happened all the time.

The baths!

I remembered the baths. In the following journal entry, I recalled intimate moments between myself, my grandmother, and my mother when she was able to visit us sometimes. Together, my grandmother and I would give my mother these sacred baths:

Primping and Preening

You want to know what love is?
I thought I knew love.
But I promise that you haven't seen love until you've watched your mother so broken, so beaten, so destroyed that you feel helpless
Oftentimes, I didn't know what to say when my mother was around
But my Grandmother always knew

My Grandmother taught me love, and she showed me love through the way that she cared for her daughter. Love is being a mother to a child who fell victim
At the height of my mother's battle with addiction, when her temperament allowed it, sometimes we could welcome her into our home for a warm meal
Grandma kept a special set of dishware for my mother whenever she came around
We knew never to eat from our mothers dishware
I would sit at the dining room table with my mother as a child
Studying her and the way she ate her food
We sat in silence most of the time, and I'd wonder where my mother's last meal came from
Sometimes she would ask me about school
I was so excited when she asked me questions
She would say 'you're so smart'
Then she would laugh, which almost turned into a deep sobbing
Conversations were difficult
I didn't know how to navigate them
I knew that she couldn't always control her laughing
So, I just sat in silence
After she ate, my Grandmother would run her a warm bath
She'd put some Epsom salt in the tub, and add some bubbles
She would take my mother's clothes, and either wash them or throw them away
We always had a drawer filled with freshly pressed, clean clothes for my mother
Whenever my mother got in that tub, she was just a splishin' and splashin'
Like she was in a swimming pool
She was a woman-child
While my mother was soaking in the tub, my grandmother got down on her knees
And she scrubbed my mother's back, as my mother bathed
My Grandmother studied her body, looking for marks
I stood by the bathroom door, watching my Grandmother care for my mother

3 generations
Bloodmother, Othermother, and the Girlchild
My grandmother cleaned and carefully clipped her fingernails
When my Grandmother grew tired of bending town to help wash my mother,
I instinctively knew to step in and take over.
When I was old enough, my Grandmother would let me help her
I just did what I knew I had to do, to help my Grandmother take care of her daughter
I needed to become the daughter who would take care of her mother
My mother would smile at me as I helped to wash her, and I would smile back
Swallowing my tears
Exhale
I really wished that she wasn't sick
I didn't want her to see me cry, because I knew that she would cry
And I knew that she couldn't really control it
So, I needed to *Shapeshift* so that I could control it for the both of us
I really wish that I got the chance to know her before she was sick
After my mother was washed, we would get her dressed and take her downstairs to the kitchen sink. I always followed behind my Grandmother.
Taking her lead.
Watching this ritual. Studying them both.
The music played on the radio by the windowsill in the kitchen
At the sink, my Grandmother would sit my mother down in a chair and scratch her scalp with a rat tail comb and her wig brush. The sensation caused my mother to hum. *"Mmmmmmm"*
My mother closed her eyes, as my Grandmother worked her magic *all up and through* my mother's scalp
My mother had a short Afro, but my Grandmother always took her time.
Shampoo, conditioner, and sometimes, she'd get the hot oil treatment under a plastic cap and hair dryer. She deserved it.

After washing her hair, my Grandmother would yell out even though I was usually standing right there,
"Yanna, go grab me the grease off the dresser upstairs in my bedroom"
And I'd go flying upstairs to get my Grandmother what she needed
Skipping every other step, so I didn't miss anything
This was love. I knew this was something special.
I enjoyed these moments
Being in the company of women
Taking care of my mother
Primping and preening
I thought I knew love
But there is nothing like this love between a mother and daughter
I smiled as I watched my mother getting nurtured
My grandmother was continuing the tradition
Despite how far my mother's addiction would take her, my grandmother's role as a mother was unbounded. Before my mother went back out into the world, we made sure that she was cleaned up and had a full belly.
Until the next time, we could welcome her back in for a hot meal and a warm bath
For some primping and preening…

In this free-write, I revisited memories of my mother's truths. I had forgotten about those baths that I would help my grandmother give my mother. How could I forget that? This particular entry started out as an audio recording, and I remember it well because I ugly cried my way through it. I started out talking about something else, and then suddenly, I remembered these baths. I do not believe that I ever talked about these baths to anyone. Ever. It wasn't anyone's business except for me, my mother, and my grandmother. I had completely forgotten about these sacred moments. This was how these moments and memories came to me, and I was finally ready to engage with these memories to reinterpret them. Finding love and grace in the chaos within the margins. I transcribed the recording and made some edits to the entry. I would remember little details here and there, and I was always fascinated by how I was engaging with all of this stuff that lay dormant inside of me for so long.

Now, I had a record of my mother's truth. It felt important like it was something that I could give to my daughters someday. This reminded me of a saying I used to share with my students, nieces, and nephews. I always told them that a short pencil was better than a long memory. I told them to always write things down so they would have a record. So they would never forget. Lessons from my othermothers. In my experience, there was so much beauty within the margins of my lived experience. These experiences and interactions often occurred within the margin.

I spent most of my adolescence traveling with my grandmother and my aunts to rehabs all around the city to visit and spend time with my mother. She liked turkey hoagies. I didn't get to see her much when I was in college, but she spent years in rehabilitation, followed by a relapse, until she was admitted into another facility to work on her rehabilitation, which was followed by a relapse. It was a vicious cycle. She had moments of sobriety—times when she was lucid enough for us to actually hold conversations together. I was older now and I didn't care how she responded to me anymore. I told her everything under the sun. I just talked to her. And she'd smile at me and tell me that I was so smart. These were all forgotten memories until now. Marginal experiences that capture how we moved forward. Amplifying the margin sheds light on aspects often overlooked. I focused on counter-narratives that emphasized vulnerability and portrayed my mother not just as a victim of circumstances but as a cherished daughter and as someone who was loved.

Through this lens, I explored my grandmother's unwavering commitment to her daughter's well-being. Despite the challenging circumstances, my grandmother consistently ensured that my mother received essential care, from warm meals to grooming and clean clothes. Black women were the operators of our homeplace, and it was my grandmother and my aunts who managed my mother's care as she hopped from one hospital to the next. Amplifying the margin tracks the truth buried in the narratives, which highlight the profound intimacy and enduring support within the Black cultural tradition of families caring for loved ones suffering from sickness, affliction, or addiction—*no matter what kind it is*!

Are you with me?

These rich traditions rarely make it to the television screens. These rich traditions are not considered when the scripts and the lyrics are being written. These rich traditions capture our truths and the resilience and strength of familial bonds, even in the face of systemic oppression and adversity. While dominant societal narratives were running their script about my mother, it was Black women who continued the tradition of self-definition by providing my mother with the care that she most certainly needed and deserved. Black women. Sisters of the yam. Salt of the Earth. Black women saved each other and everyone else.

Exhale.

Applying The Sankofa Writing Method

Affirmation
I honor and cherish the legacy of my ancestors, recognizing their resilience and their sacrifices.

Putting Concepts into Action
In this chapter, we capture our ancestors from a holistic view by amplifying marginal experiences which center the voices of the oppressed. Through the process of amplifying our ancestors' truth, I explore the imperative of correcting and making right the narratives that have been silenced or misrepresented while honoring their humanity. By amplifying the marginal experiences from my childhood, I elevate my mother's story, which is that she was cared for, catered to, cherished, nurtured, pampered, and protected by our family. Beauty resides in the margins. The business of redressing our ancestors requires us to acknowledge their victimhood and honor their humanity amidst the adversity they faced. I've shared my truth. Now it's your turn.

Gratitude Meditation Exercises

Find a comfortable and quiet place to sit or lie down. Close your eyes and take a few deep breaths to center yourself. Think of someone or something you are deeply grateful for.

It could be an ancestor, a loved one, a friend, or a cherished memory. As you focus on this person or thing, allow yourself to fully experience the feelings of gratitude and appreciation. Notice any sensations in your body, such as warmth, openness, or lightness.

Now, silently repeat a series of phrases expressing gratitude towards this person or thing.

You can use phrases like:

"Thank you for being a part of my life."

"I am grateful for the love and support you provide."

"Your presence brings me joy and happiness."

Continue to repeat these phrases, allowing them to resonate deeply within you.

Stay in this state of gratitude for as long as you feel comfortable

When you are ready to conclude the meditation, take a few more deep breaths and slowly bring your awareness back to the present moment.

Open your eyes and carry the sense of gratitude with you as you go about your day.

Mapping the Margins of Our Ancestors' Truths

It is time to shift marginal experiences so that we may position them back to their proper subject place. It is time to shift them to the center. In the chart below, rewrite the list of your beliefs about your ancestors to honor their truth. You can use words or phrases like *"cared for," "loved by many,"* and you can describe them as *"beautiful."* In my chart, I wrote down that my mother is a grandmother. Although she transitioned many years ago, it does not make this truth any less of a truth. My children know of their grandmother Tremayne, so it is important for me to capture this identifier as her truth. I also used words like *creative, animal lover, beautiful, impulsive, musician, deep thinker, big sister, little sister, Aunt, giver, kind, expressive, playful, trusting,* and *innocent.*

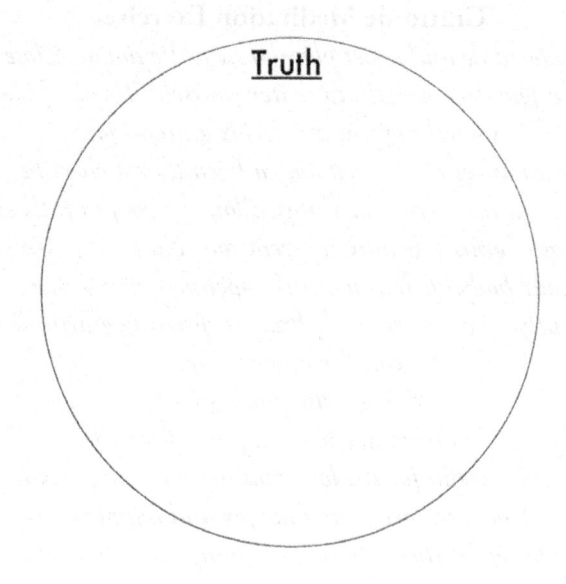

(circle diagram labeled "Truth")

Writing Prompts

- ❖ Identify and reflect on marginal experiences and moments when your ancestor experienced being cared for, joy, pleasure, and love as empowering and validating experiences.
- ❖ What new insights or perspectives have you gained about amplifying marginalized experiences through this chapter?
- ❖ How can we continue to challenge and disrupt harmful narratives about addiction in popular culture?
- ❖ Consider the idea of reframing marginal positions in your own life. Are there narratives or beliefs about yourself or your family history that you would like to correct or challenge?
- ❖ In what ways can storytelling and narratives be used as tools for social justice and inclusivity in conversations about addiction and recovery?
- ❖ What emotions arise for you when considering the humanity of individuals who struggle with addiction, particularly in the context of personal relationships?

Chapter 7
Go Free, Wildflower

I'm a big fan of Black women because in our blood is space travel. Because we come from an unknown. Through an unknown. To an unknown. Black women know space travel. And that's all that space travel is. If anybody can find what there is in this darkness, it's Black women.
~ Nikki Giovanni

You have done it. You've reached a significant milestone in your journey toward healing and reclaiming the truth of your ancestors. You've done the hardest part, and now, it's time to *write to transgress*—it's time to cross over. In this chapter, we embark on the last phase of the Sankofa Writing Method, where we harness the power of our radical imaginations to reimagine a counter-future for our ancestors. In this chapter, we create peace and calm for our mothers, who birthed us.

In this chapter, you should take all of the information, and the realizations you've gathered during each step of this process to *write your ancestor free!* In this exercise, you will now use Black speculative fiction and Afrofuturist conventions to reimagine your ancestor and their progressive future. Use what you've learned about the writing characteristics of the Sankofa Writing Method by using the toolkit provided in Chapter two.

The essence of this chapter lies in utilizing your radical imagination to craft narratives that transcend the limitations imposed by the white gaze. The Sankofa Writing Method serves as a freedom device and a decolonizing tool of liberation, offering strategies to empower individuals to reshape their own narratives. Reimagining holds transformative potential as a healing mechanism, inviting us to creatively envision alternative histories, perspectives, and possibilities. Through this process, we can transcend the confines of past traumas and reimagine ourselves and our ancestors in new, empowering contexts. This chapter invites you to release the grip of *critical traumatic incidents* that have occupied significant space in your life, and to recreate those spaces with intention and purpose.

It's time to release these moments.

Clear out these memories that no longer serve you!

Dust it out.

Sage it down!

Are you ready?

Your goal is to write until you feel like you can't write anymore

Wildflower Excerpt

Below is an excerpt of my mother's story—where I use a *critical traumatic incident* from my childhood to reimagine her as a *Wildflower*:

Wash Day

> We are gathered at the meeting place, and my mother watches me from the front steps of my grandmother's home. We're getting ready to play hopscotch, and we just finished drawing the outline of the game in the middle of the street with a piece of chalk. The chalk is everywhere—all over our hands and clothes. Nobody minds. It's warm and humid outside, and the block is filled with people and kids running up and down the street. My daughters run circles around each other—the beads in their hair—clinking and clanking like

maracas. As we prepare for the game, my girlchildren begin to bicker about who gets to go first. Kids. My mother sits quietly, observing the interaction, legs crossed and smiling at us, sipping on her tea and blowing smoke clouds from her bamboo smoke holder—plant medicine. I roll my eyes at the sound of the children fussing, and I return her smile. From the house, I can hear Santana blasting loudly through the open windows—pouring from the speakers in the living room into the street.
Vinyl records spinning on a copper-plated turntable.
Cinnamon incense burning.
Sending sweet and spicy aroma all up and through the meeting place.
My mother closes her eyes briefly and changes the song without lifting a finger. "Black Magic Woman/Gypsy Queen" fills up the space. My mother is a composer, a lover of all music, with eclectic taste. Like a moth to a flame, she's drawn to the syncopation. Her eyes closed now; she enjoys the melodic tempo coming from the speakers. She sways back and forth, kicks drum foot taps over rhythmic beats. Chimes ringing from her wrists through finger taps on her right knee. Her aura—serene. Her thoughts are briefly interrupted as my eldest daughter, Jordan, shouts out that she should go first because she's the oldest. Kids. My youngest, Ava, yells and screams, "that's not fair!" The girlchildren stop bickering abruptly as they stand still in the street, looking toward my mother. Her eyes are still closed—and they both say, "Sorry, Grandma""
Downloads flowing through the bloodline.

I begin to explain the rules of the game. I share that in this game, their grandmother actually goes first. Lessons on deference. My daughters squeal with excitement. My mother laughs from the step—a laugh so deep and so contagious that you can't help but return her laugh. She obliges and tells her granddaughters that she would be honored to play the game with us. She stands up—putting down her tea, and smoke holder before she walks over to us.
Wildflower emerging.
My mother's stature is tall, and her skin—creamy and smooth— just like her mother's. Honey complected—with razor-sharp dark brown eyes. Eyes seeing through everyone. Her walk, manifesting a

Rimshot—reverberating sharp, crisp vibrations on the concrete with every stride. Let's go Mom! Affirmations to match her frequency. I give her a high five as she nears me. Her presence is percussive. You can hear her coming—chimes clanking from the charm bracelets dangling from her wrists. Her hair is shiny, black, and thick. She wears it in a long underbraid, going down the spine of her back, tickling her hamstrings, all the way down to her ankles. Her braid is adorned with ornate gemstone beads and charms. She grabs her hair, and in one swift-swoop, she wraps it in a bun—creating a crown to avoid tripping on her hair during the game.

She looks at her granddaughters—sharp glances and guidance exchanged. My daughters reply, "Yes mam," and they wrap their long braids too—creating honeycomb buns on the top of their crowns. I follow suit and wrap my own hair.

Blackmothers, Bloodmothers, and Girlchildren taking up space— twirling our braids and adjusting our crowns in the middle of the street.

My mother tells my daughters to watch out as she begins to take aim on the hopscotch grid that we've outlined on the street. My daughters are so giddy, and they yell "Go Grandma" from the curb as they watch my mother hop-step-hop her way through the grid. She takes her turn, and then we go round and round. Neighbors join in on the amusement, watching us from their porches. The sun is high, and it's such a warm day. We end the game when my youngest daughter wins! Ava prances around the street—screaming "I won, I won!"—and we all laugh.

My mother hugs her granddaughters tight—she loves tight, long hugs. We all do. We used hugs in our family for their healing, restorative power. Lifting vibrations and filling one another up. The three of them huddled in a circle. Eyes closed as they gathered quietly in front of the meeting place. Sacred rituals. I observe my mother's expression as she smiles and holds them tight. My girlchildren stand quietly as they listen to their grandmother's thoughts.

I stand back—averting my glance to give them space. I hear a beautiful tune, and I spot a green hummingbird circling over us—she was smiling at me. I returned her smile, closed my eyes, and I could feel my grandmother's presence—I could hear her satisfaction from her aerial view—singing songs of adoration and strength. I could feel her. Her presence is warm. Holding me tight. Moments pass and then my girlchildren burst into laughter suddenly. All of us opening our eyes. My girlchildren jump up and down with excitement. My mother held their hands and walked them back over to the meeting place, and picked up a basket that was sitting near the front door.

Inside of the basket were gemstone charm bracelets, flowers, an assortment of their favorite candies, and sets of glasses that were filled with recordings of their favorite movies and songs. "Thank you, thank you Grandma," they yelled. She looked at me and smiled, extending her hand toward mine and mouthing to me that they were simply beautiful. I reached her grasp with my hand, squeezed tight, and responded, "Thank you, Mom. So are you."

She glanced at Jordan, and Jordan responded—"Okay!" before flying into the house to retrieve whatever her grandmother asked of her. We gathered at the meeting place, listening to the bongos, Afro-Cuban rhythms—improvisation blending with blues, jazz, rock, African and Latin sounds. We were grooving—and Ava danced on the sidewalk. Jordan returned with an orange pillow and a chrome-plated box—adorned with shells and filled with combs, brushes, essential oils, hair ties, and beads.

My mother sat at the top of the steps next to her tea and bamboo smoke holder.

She spread her legs to give me room to sit between her thighs.
I sat down on the next step, spreading my legs to give my eldest girlchild room to sit between my thighs. She placed the pillow down on the last step, then she sat down and made room for my youngest girlchild to sit between her thighs.
Then Ava sat at the bottom of the steps, legs crossed—Indian style—grabbing her pair of glasses out of the basket that was gifted to her moments before by her grandmother. The hummingbird circled us from above, singing a beautiful song, as my mother passed rattail combs down to her girlchildren. We got to work—understanding our assignment.

Today was Wash Day.

Working meticulously to take down our crowns, our braids, and our beads so that we can spend the rest of our day massaging each other's scalps, washing and re-braiding our hair.
Continuing the tradition—just like our Queen Mother Kathleen taught us.

This text captures a draft of one of my initial attempts at rewriting my mother's narrative as a *Wildflower*. My goal was to write at least one page. This was challenging at first for me to try and describe my mother's counter-future. I entered this story being intentional about setting the scene through the selection of a *critical traumatic incident*—the one about the stolen tapes. I chose to start from my pain so that I could reclaim and rewrite this memory as a new one that amplified joy. I used all the nuggets of wisdom that I collected while applying the Sankofa Writing Method. I incorporated my mother's personality traits, her passions, her pleasures, and her hobbies. I wanted to play with elements of bending time.

My mother transitioned five years before I gave birth to my eldest daughter, Jordan. This was a pain point for me that I intentionally wanted to explore. This process forced me to grieve my mother's absence in my life and my children's lives. While writing my mother's futurity, it meant the world to be able to see my daughter's names tied to my mother's names within the same text on a page. Something happened when I described the warm embrace between a grandmother and a granddaughter. I wrote from a place of remembrance, recalling how safe those hugs from my own grandmother made me feel.

Through this process, I was creating restoration between bloodlines and generations through my writing and imagination. In this draft, I was not yet ready to fully give my mother her voice. I wrote about her in third person, and I did not think too much about this as I was writing this initial draft. Writing about my mother this way came naturally. I needed to create distance between us as I played with elements of my mother engaging with her granddaughters. I knew that I would recreate many intimate moments between my mother and I eventually, and fully restore her voice. For now—I chose to focus on her interactions with her grandchildren. In addition to playing with elements of bending time, I wanted to create an intimate connection between my children and my mother—similar to the connection that I had with my own grandmother.

My grandmother and I spoke our own language, and so much of what I learned from her were lessons that were never verbally discussed. We spoke with one another through our eyes and our minds. I knew what my grandmother needed and wanted before she ever needed to speak a word. *Shapeshifters*—Black women using telepathy to send urgent messages to their girlchildren through our thoughts and non-verbal expressions. So, I sought to speculatively recreate this intergenerational interaction by playing with my mother's ability to communicate with her grandchildren through their thoughts. Sacred moments and secrets between granddaughters and their grandmother. Secrets that were no one else's business but theirs. Similarly, wash day was another sacred tradition between Black women and girls. Sitting between the legs of our *Bloodmothers, Othermothers, and BigSisters* was a rite of passage for Black girlchildren growing up. No matter where you were from, no matter what neighborhood you were raised in, no matter how much education you had, no matter what your hair texture was like—getting our crowns done by another Black woman was a ritual in our homeplace a cultural tradition.

I spent much of my girlhood getting my hair done by my grandmother and my aunts—yet I still yearned for my own mother to do my hair. How I wished that she could scratch my scalp, braid my hair, and tell me stories of her childhood. An exchange that, unfortunately—could never occur. But that's quite alright—I was *Shapeshifting* and radically reimagining new futures for us, so I would create a safe space for my mother and me to engage in this sacred ritual. I knew that I could write it—a deliberate act of continuing the tradition. So, I did. As I reflect on this early draft as a moment of restoration, I am struck by the profound impact of storytelling in reclaiming our ancestral truths. By reimagining my mother's narrative as a *Wildflower*, I am not only honoring her memory but also forging a path toward healing and reconciliation.

This practice of writing my mother as a *Wildflower* was symbolic, spiritual, and healing for me. I no longer hold space for any negative thoughts about my mother. I have moments where I feel guilty about my response to her all of those years and for the time that I lost with her. The healing process is a journey, and I try not to wallow in these moments for too long. I give myself grace by acknowledging what I was able to accomplish in the retelling of my mother's story. This process has been transformational for me, and the beliefs that I once had about my mother stemming from my childhood are no longer valid. I *Shapeshifted* to heal myself. I needed to be able to tell my daughters who their grandmother was, based on *her* truth. Through the power of imagination, I was able to weave together the threads of our shared history, stitching together ruptured generations with love and compassion. In rewriting our stories, we have the opportunity to break free from the chains of intergenerational and cultural trauma and envision counter-futures filled with hope and possibility. With each word penned, we continue the tradition and take steps towards healing, restoring the resilience and strength that have been passed down through the ages. We continue the tradition.

Carry it on now. Carry it on. Carry it on now. Carry it on.
…Pass it down to the children. Pass it down. Carry it on. Carry it on now. Carry it on
TO FREEDOM!

- Assata Shakur

Applying The Sankofa Writing Method

Affirmation

The legacy of my ancestors lives on through me as I embrace their teachings and carry their love forward.

Putting Concepts into Action
Now, it's your turn to apply what you've learned. Use what you've learned about the writing characteristics of the Sankofa Writing Method in Chapter two. Through your creative storytelling, you can blend elements of science fiction, fantasy, mythology, African futurity, and your ancestor's truth to envision bold and imaginative futures:

Grounding Meditation Exercise

Hold your mother in your mind for a few minutes
Think of her
Imagine her free
What languages does she speak?
What does her hair look like?
Is she alone, or is she with another ancestor?
What is she doing?
What is she wearing?
How old is she?
What are her superpowers?
What's her favorite color?
Does she prefer Kale or Collards?
Where does she like to go?
What are her secrets?
What gives her pleasure?
Who does she spend her time with?
What planet would she visit?
Where does she live?
What does she like to eat/drink?
What is her personality like?
What would she tell you?

Writing Prompts

- ❖ With these reflections in mind, begin to write freely. Allow your thoughts and emotions to flow onto the page, guided by the imagery you just created through this grounding exercise.
- ❖ You can choose to reimagine a counter-history or future by using one of the *critical traumatic incidents* you identified in Chapter three: Excavating Truth. The objective here is to replace the traumatic event with an alternative version that centers on your ancestor's liberation and resilience.
- ❖ You may choose to reimagine a counter-history or future from scratch that is not tied to any specific event in your life. You may choose to write what feels organic for you.
- ❖ As you rewrite each narrative, infuse it with all the nuggets of truths you collected along your journey. Incorporate everything! This is your opportunity to make *Wildflower gumbo*!
- ❖ This process has been heavy, but now that we're on the side of it, it is time to create. Using all that's been collected, begin to *write your ancestor free*!
- ❖ Last but certainly not least. Go off!

Closing Reflections

It is imperative that we, as Black women, talk about the experiences that shaped us; that we assess our strengths and weaknesses and define our own history. It is imperative that we discuss positive ways to teach and socialize our children... Let us rebuild the culture of giving and carry on the tradition of fierce determination to move on closer to freedom.
- Assata Shakur

Moving Forward

We made it. You made it. You've journeyed through the depths of freedom dreaming, healing, and growth. You *Shapeshifted* so that you could heal yourself. You've reached the other side, and I couldn't be more proud of you. You've done the difficult and daunting work of acknowledging your shadow and confronting your cultural trauma. Not only that—you've rewritten it. You've reshaped the narrative, reclaiming agency for yourself and your ancestors. Through your courage and resilience, you've reframed the context in which your trauma existed. You destroyed the myths and amplified the margins. You did this, and you did not need anyone's permission to do so except for your own. This is an incredible achievement, and I applaud your bravery, and your vulnerability.

The Sankofa Writing Method has been transformative in my life and has completely shifted my perspective. It has changed how I think about my mother, other Black women, and other Black and Brown people who truly were victims of this American tragedy and other forms of cultural trauma. This process has changed how I talk about my mother; it has changed how I talk about my mother to my children. As a scholar, it has shifted my perspectives on how we examine divergent or marginal experiences and narratives within historical contexts. I believe there's healing in truth. For me, my personal healing journey enabled me to combine my love for scholarship, art, creative writing, and theorizing to develop a culturally informed speculative framework that will help others to heal.

Thank you for joining me on this journey. Gratitude for trusting me and allowing me to share pieces of my truth to track how I came to this work.

Now that you've completed this process, it's time to decide what comes next. For some, internal healing may be sufficient, and there's no obligation to share your story with others. You may decide that your work here is done. For those who feel called to share, consider this an opportunity to initiate conversations with loved ones or family members. Use your experience and the tools provided in this book as a starting point for dialogue. Your story can serve as a portal to healing for others, offering them insight and understanding into their own experiences.

As you embark on this next phase of your journey, remember that your ability to impact others is directly linked to your willingness to dig deep. By sharing your truth, you have the power to heal and inspire those around you. Some may even feel compelled to follow in your footsteps and share their own stories of healing and resilience. To those who are ready to take the bold step of sharing their stories, I invite you to join me in healing others. Let us be disruptors, reclaiming our ancestral tongues and empowering others through the power of storytelling. Together, we can create a ripple effect of healing and transformation that extends far beyond ourselves.

> *"For Black people, the past is painful, the present precarious, but the future is free. Black people have always seen themselves in the future"*
>
> *~ Erika Alexander*

Healing Through Storytelling

The methods and framework outlined in this book serve as a portal for healing those impacted by some form of cultural trauma, offering a transformative journey toward healing and reclaiming ancestral narratives. Through the Sankofa Writing Method, it is my hope that readers are guided on a path of deep healing and connection to their roots through storytelling. This book honors the resilience and wisdom of our foremothers, highlighting the importance of remembering and honoring their legacy. At its core, the book emphasizes the power of storytelling as a decolonizing tool for healing and community building. By sharing our stories, we not only validate our lived experiences but also contribute to a collective narrative of strength and resilience.

The importance of being witnessed and validated in one's healing journey is underscored, highlighting the significance of creating spaces for connection and support. Writing this book has transformed me by deepening my connection to my own ancestral narratives and fostering a greater sense of empathy and understanding. It has empowered me to reclaim my voice and share my truth with the world.

Moreover, this book invites readers to engage in actionable steps towards healing, such as sharing their stories with trusted individuals or participating in storytelling circles. These practices foster a sense of empowerment and resilience, allowing readers to reclaim agency over their narratives and rewrite their own stories. It is my fervent wish that readers walk away feeling seen, empowered, validated, and have a deeper connection to their ancestors. Your story matters and you have the power to create positive change in the world.

Embrace your story.

Honor your ancestors.

Walk boldly in the power of your truth.

You are enough.

You are worthy and deserving of healing and love!

Applying The Sankofa Writing Method

Affirmation

I cultivate inner peace and resilience, embracing my heritage as a source of strength and healing

Putting Concepts into Action

As we go forward, we continue the tradition. This is the essence of quilt work, as we recreate new narratives under new suns. We stand as proverbial botanists, sowing seeds of wisdom and strength into the hearts of our children. This profound healing journey calls us to remember the ancient guidance of our foremothers, who have laid the groundwork for our resilience in times of adversity. Let us continue their legacy through the radical act of storytelling, healing, and community building. Together, let us continue to cultivate a community of healing, strength, and empowerment. Your story is a vital thread in the fabric of our collective resilience.

Reflections & Next Steps

- ❖ Reflect on your healing journey and the insights gained through the Sankofa Writing Method. Write about how you have integrated these insights into your life and relationships.
- ❖ How do you envision your future now that you have taken intentional steps towards your journey in healing and reclaiming your ancestral narratives?
- ❖ How has using Black speculative fiction and Afrofuturist elements empowered you to reimagine the lives of your ancestors and envision futures free from oppression?

- ❖ Reflect on the profound experience of being witnessed and validated in your healing journey. How does sharing your stories contribute to your sense of connection and resilience?
- ❖ Take a courageous step forward by sharing your stories with trusted friends, family members, or a clinical professional.
- ❖ Create healing spaces within your own family and social networks to start dialogue free from judgment about your loved ones.

Flowerchild

Mother
I'm taking back what's yours
You are my wildflower, and I am your flowerchild
I never would have imagined that *this* is how I would enter the retelling of our story
Did you know this when you selected my name?
Sending coded messages through the birth canal
Of course, you did
I am grateful and I honor you as my ancestor
Asé
I am grateful to all of my ancestors for teaching me discernment to recognize divine timing
Asé
I am grateful to my ancestors for preparing me to do this work
Asé
I am grateful to my ancestors for teaching me to speak up - throat chakra strong
Asé
I am grateful to my ancestors for guiding me and gifting me a short pencil and a long memory
Asé
I am grateful to my ancestors for teaching me how to wonder and pull stars out of the sky
Asé

I am grateful to my ancestors for granting me with the ability to interpret phenomena, patterns and generate new ideas to shape and contribute towards intellectual discourse
Asé
I am grateful to my ancestors for holding me tight and armoring me for this fight
Asé
I am grateful to journey forth towards healing and creating new ways of knowing so that we can heal and better understand ourselves
Asé
I am grateful to my ancestors for giving me permission to retell their stories
Asé
I am grateful to my ancestors for teaching me that 'I am because we are'
Asé
I am grateful for the wisdom bestowed upon my girlchild, who at 4 years old, would ignite a spark that would allow me to see my mother's sacrifice, and use my pain to spark a feminist uprising
Asé
I am grateful for the urgent messages and distress calls sent through the bloodline
Asé

Exhale.

I am grateful that the next time one of my girlchildren asks me who my mother is.
I won't have to wonder.
I'll know.
Asé

Medicine Cabinet

This project tracks my healing journey, and throughout this text, I shared the medicine, the antidotes, the cures, the castor oil, the cod liver oil, and the remedies that helped me to remember, recover, and move forward. Throughout this text, I share the literary herbs from my bookshelf—manifested as medicinal data and antioxidant epistemological ponderings – that helped me to heal. Sacred text wrapped in rosemary, witch-hazel, sage, nutmeg, and thyme. I shared the scholarship in my medicine cabinet. Like the Black women Shapeshifters who saved me and raised me—I wish to share these remedies with others who aspire to go deep in their healing journeys to also remember, recover, and move forward.

Citational cider for the soul.

- ❖ Asante, M. K. (1987). The Afrocentric Idea. Temple University Press.
- ❖ Asante, M. K. (2003). Afrocentricity: The Theory of Social Change (revised and expanded). African American Images.
- ❖ Baker-Bell, A. (2017). For Loretta: A Black woman literacy scholar's journey to prioritizing self-preservation and Black feminist–womanist storytelling. *Journal of Literacy Research, 49*(4), 526-543.
- ❖ Boylorn, R. M. (2014). From here to there: How to use auto/ethnography to bridge difference. *International Review of Qualitative Research, 7*(3), 312-326.
- ❖ Boylorn, R. M. (2016). On being at home with myself: Blackgirl autoethnography as research praxis. *International Review of Qualitative Research, 9*(1), 44-58.
- ❖ Boylorn, R. M. (2013). Blackgirl blogs, auto/ethnography, and crunk feminism. *Liminalities: A Journal of Performance Studies, 9*(2), 73-82.
- ❖ Butler, Octavia E. (1980). *Wild Seed.* Grand Central Publishing.
- ❖ Collins, P.H. (1990). *Black feminist thought: Knowledge, consciousness, and the politics of empowerment.* Routledge.

- Dillard, Cynthia B. (2012). *Learning to (Re)member the Things We've Learned to Forget: Endarkened Feminisms, Spirituality, and the Sacred Nature of Research and Teaching.* Black Studies Critical Thinking, Volume 18. Peter Lang, New York.
- Dillard, Cynthia B. (2000). "The substance of things hoped for, the evidence of things not seen: Examining an endarkened feminist epistemology in educational research and leadership." *International journal of qualitative studies in education, 13*(6), 661-681.
- Evans-Winters, Venus E. (2019). *Black feminism in qualitative inquiry: A mosaic for writing our daughter's body.* Routledge.
- Giovanni, Nikki. (2002). *Quilting the Black-Eyed Pea: Poems and Not Quite Poems.* HarperCollins.
- Hardaway, A. T., Ward, L. W., & Howell, D. (2019). Black girls and womyn matter: Using Black feminist thought to examine violence and erasure in education. *Urban Education Research & Policy Annuals, 6*(1).
- Hardaway, A.T., (2024). Quilting the Black-Eyed Pea: Exploring Endarkened Afrofuturist Feminism & Shapeshifting in Octavia E. Butler's "Wild Seed" In: *Introduction to Afrofuturism: A Mixtape in Black Literature & Arts* (Eds) Frazier, D.
- Hartman, S. (2008). Venus in two acts. *Small Axe: A Caribbean Journal of Criticism, 12*(2), 1-14.
- Hartman, S. (2019). *Wayward Lives, Beautiful Experiments: Intimate Histories of Riotous Black Girls, Troublesome Women, and Queer Radicals.* W. W. Norton & Company.
- Hersey, T. (2022). Rest is resistance: a manifesto. Little, Brown Spark.
- hooks, b. (1990). *Homeplace: A Site of Resistance.* Routledge.
- hooks, b. (1994). *Teaching to Transgress: Education as the Practice of Freedom.* Routledge.
- hooks, b. (1989). *Talking Back: Thinking Feminist, Thinking Black.* South End Press.

- hooks, b. (2000). *Feminist theory: From margin to center.* Pluto Press.
- hooks, b. (1993). *Sisters of the Yam: Black Women and Self-Recovery.* South End Press.
- Morris, Susana M. (2012). Black Girls Are from the Future: Afrofuturist Feminism in Octavia E. Butler's *Fledgling. Women's Studies Quarterly, 40*(3/4), 146-166.
- Ramsey, D. X. (2023). When Crack Was King: A People's History of a Misunderstood Era. One World.
- Roberts, D. (2014). *Killing the black body: Race, reproduction, and the meaning of liberty.* Vintage.
- Semmes, C. E. (1981). Foundations of an Afrocentric social science: Implications for curriculum-building, theory, and research in black studies. *Journal of Black Studies, 12*(1), 3-17.
- Sharpe, T. T. (2005). *Behind the Eight Ball: Sex for Crack Cocaine Exchange and Poor Black Women.* Haworth Press.
- Smith, Aaron X., and Molefi Kete Asante. *Afrocentricity in Afrofuturism: Toward Afrocentric Futurism.* University Press of Mississippi, 2023.
- Toliver, Stephanie R. *Recovering Black storytelling in qualitative research: Endarkened*
- *storywork.* Routledge, 2021.
- Therapist Aid LLC. (2021). *Cognitive Triangle.* Retrieved from https://www.therapistaid.com/therapy-worksheet/cbt-triangle
- Welsing, F. C. (1991). *The Isis Papers: The Keys to the Colors.* C.W. Publishing.

About the Author

Dr. Ayana T. Hardaway is a writer, scholar, theorist, creative, and storyteller. Her research explores Black feminisms, cultural trauma, Black speculative methodology, critical qualitative inquiry, and higher education. She earned her M.Ed. and Ph.D. in Urban Education from Temple University. Her work has appeared in ***Introduction to Afrofuturism: A Mixtape in Black Literature & Arts***, ***Journal of African American Women and Girls in Education***, and ***Investing in the Education Success of Black Women and Girls***. Hardaway is a Philadelphia native and currently resides in San Diego with her family.

ayanathardaway.com

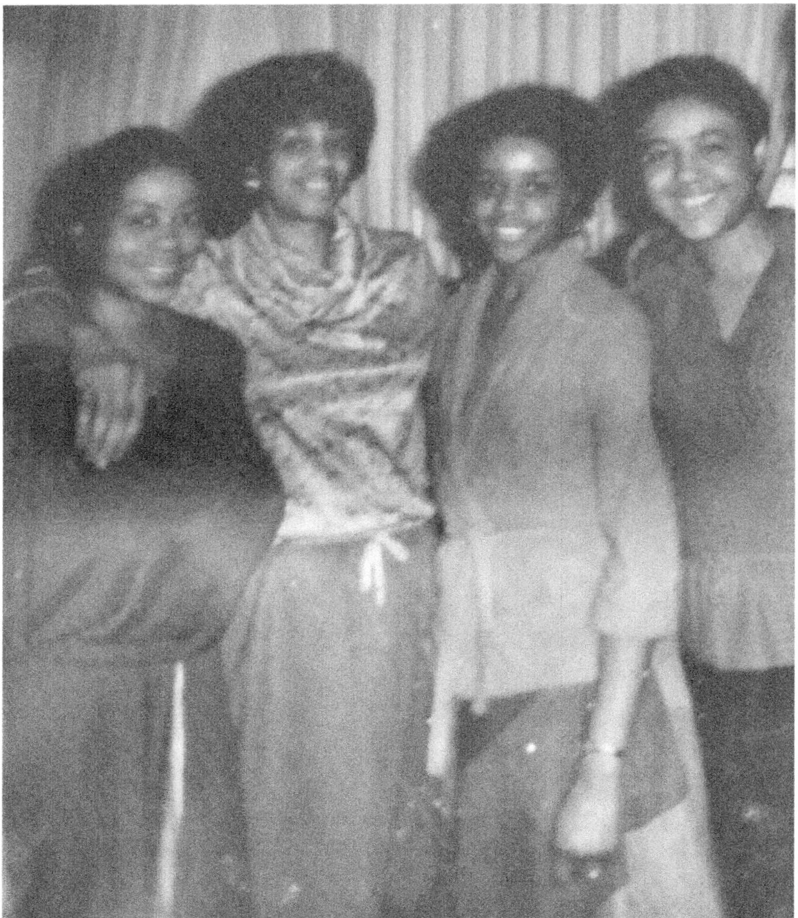

Made in the USA
Monee, IL
20 September 2024